ICT 사회 연구 총서 4

iCat
정보기술과문화연구소

Digital Technology and the Change of Social Life

Digital Korea

EDITED BY Wooyeol Shin, Kyung-Hee Kim, & Changwook Kim

한울
아카데미

First published in 2018 by HanulMplus Inc.

HanulMplus Inc.
153, Gwanginsa-gil, Paju-si, Gyeonggi-do, 10881, Republic of Korea

ISBN 978-89-460-7078-3 93300

This work was supported by the Ministry of Education of the Republic of Korea and the
National Research Foundation of Korea(NRF-2015S1A5B4A01037022).

이 도서의 국립중앙도서관 출판예정도서목록(CIP)은 서지정보유통지원시스템 홈페이지(http://seoji.nl.go.kr)와
국가자료공동목록시스템(http://www.nl.go.kr/kolisnet)에서 이용하실 수 있습니다.
(CIP제어번호: CIP2018017725)

Contents

The Structural Development of the Public Sphere in Korea

1

WOOYEOL SHIN

The Korea Center for Investigative Journalism

The 2008 Korean Candlelight Vigil was a massive social movement held by Korean citizens against the conservative Lee Myung-Bak government and its policies. The protesters were mostly young liberal-progressives in their twenties and thirties (K. Cho, 2009). In Korea, liberal-progressives are generally described as follows: democratic, highly nationalistic, humanitarian, advocating "a mixed economy or democratically planned economic model that increases welfare, encourages fair participation of all people in production processes, and ensures economic freedom" (Steinberg & Shin, 2006). They also prefer an independent foreign policy and show opposition to the U.S. involvement in the politics of the Korean peninsula (Chae & Kim, 2008).

During more than six decades after the liberation from Japanese colonial rule in 1945, Korean liberal-progressives have been marginalized by mainstream politics. Democratization in Korea has been a "conservative process" that failed to include the interests of the progressive or left-wing movements and of everyday citizens into mainstream politics (Choi, 2005). The state and conservative parties have continuously used the anti-communism or anti-Americanism rhetoric as a justification for their oppression against civil society (K. Cho, 1997; Kraft, 2008). Through a series of historical events—

such as Japanese colonization, national liberation, the U.S. military occupation, the foundation of the Republic of Korea, the division of the Korean peninsula, the Korean War and its resultant devastation, a period of economic development, three decades of military dictatorship, and the transition to democracy—and the ways that the state has dealt with these events, those Koreans born in the 1930s and 1940s have deeply internalized anti-communism and pro-Americanism and equated these ideologies with national security and public safety (Lee, 2007: 70–108). Many efforts to introduce reform and progressive ideologies into the political process in Korea therefore have been viewed as left-wing and pro-communist and thus subversive (Lee, 2007). The Korean conservatives have argued that it is wrong to criticize the United States. In their opinion, without the long-standing U.S-South Korea alliance, Korea would have never experienced rapid economic growth on its own (Doucette, 2012). These meanings and values have become the basis of Korean conservatism and prevailed in Korean society.

In this process, the mainstream media have colluded with the conservative forces, and this collusive relationship has helped maintain the conservative dominance in the public sphere in Korea. In particular, the conservative forces have used the news media for solving political problems and justifying their suppression of the opposing groups (Park, Kim, & Sohn, 2000). The conservative forces have still reduced the autonomy of the news media vis-à-vis the state and thus provoked their lack of credibility. This historical context can be traced to political and economic structures of the media system, occupational codes and organizational routines of daily journalism, and literary forms that journalists work with.

The conservative dominance in the news media has hampered the legitimacy of the public sphere and ultimately continued to invite civil society to seek alternative forms of expression and communication. Korean citizens have continuously challenged the conservative dominant public sphere through developing alternative media system. Particularly, since the Internet emerged as a new platform for social interaction, Korean liberal-progressives have appropriated the Internet to participate in civic actions. This progressive appropriation of the Internet has contributed to the rise and changing characteristics of collective civic action in Korea. The case of the 2008 Korean Candlelight Vigil should be also explained within the broader context of the liberal-progressives' struggles to transform political power structure in Korean society.

This chapter explores how the process of developing the relationships among the state, civil society, and media system has influenced the flow of information in the public sphere in Korea. This chapter focuses on (1) how the mainstream news companies have colluded with the conservative and business imperatives; (2) how the conservative-dominated media system has helped to extend and rationalize the conservative forces' domination over the liberal-progressives; (3) how the liberal-progressives have struggled to foster diversity in media discourse through developing alternative media systems; (4) how the liberal-progressives have appropriated the Internet to participate in political actions; and (5) how these processes have been connected to the emergence of the 2008 Korean Candlelight Vigil.

THE BIRTH OF CONSERVATISM IN THE KOREAN MEDIA SYSTEM

The Two Military Regimes between 1961 and 1988 and their Control on the Media

In Korea, there is a long-lasting collusive relationship among the state, capital, and media system. Many scholars have made the critique that this collusive relationship has continued to severely hamper democratic consolidation in Korea (Park et al., 2000). These close relationships were developed and reinforced under the rule of two military authoritarian regimes—the Park regime (1961–1979) and the Chun regime (1980–1988). Ironically, many media companies achieved more social and political power due to media control by this authoritarian political power (Park et al., 2000: 120).

Under the rule of two military authoritarian regimes between 1961 and 1988, the state wielded enormous power over civil society, and the people barely enjoyed their political rights and civil liberties. The news media were controlled and supervised by the government. The violation of the freedom of press by the military regimes was fundamental due to "the nonexistence of a system of checks and balances in the Korean political system" (Yang, 2005: 22). In particular, the news media was viewed as a tool for social integration and control of the public and for achieving rapid modernization.

During his eighteen-year rule (1961–1979), Park Chung-Hee, who came to power through a coup d'état, repressed the news organizations in broad and fundamental ways through the change in the media system. The government imposed severe media restrictions through the Declaration of the State of National Emergency, and Martial Law Decree, which banned "all indoor and outdoor assemblies and demonstrations for the purpose of political activities and speeches, publications, press and broadcasts" (Youm, 1996: 55). In addition, the regime forced journalists who were critical of the dictator Park to resign. As a result, in 1975, 134 reporters were fired from the *Dong-A Ilbo*, and 33 reporters were fired from the *Chosun Ilbo* (Park et al., 2000: 100). Through removing such "obstacles," the state could weaken the critical functions of the press and control it more effectively.

Park's dictatorship ended with his death by assassination in 1979. At that time, Korean people believed that the dictator's death would bring about the recovery of democracy (Yoon, 2010: 19). However, Park's protégés in the Republic of Korea (ROK) Army launched another coup d'état and replaced the Park's regime with one of their own. In 1980, the new military regime amended the Constitution of the Republic of Korea in order to justify its authority, and as planned, a ROK Army general, Chun Doo-Hwan, became the President of South Korea. Chun and his followers were associated with massive human rights violations, including interrogation, torture, execution, or exile (Yoon, 2010).

Chun Doo-Hwan also severely restricted the press. In July and August 1980, the Chun's government conducted an unprecedented "Purification Campaign" against the press, "focusing a sweeping structural reorganization of the Korean news media" (Yang, 2005: 21). Under the purification campaign, 172 periodicals were banned and approximately 870 journalists were dismissed from their positions. In addition, in November 1980, the Chun regime forcefully merged the newspaper and broadcasting companies, and consequently, only one newspaper organization was licensed to publish a newspaper for each province, except in the Seoul area (Park et al., 2000: 113). In addition, six major private news agencies were merged into the *Yonhap News Agency*. Along with this structural reorganization of the mass media, the Chun regime enacted The Basic Press Act of 1980, which was the legal symbol of Chun regime's media control. The law justified the government's censorship and control over newspapers, periodicals, and broadcast media (Youm, 1996).

While the press was used as a tool to justify the governments' authoritarian rules, the news media gained political and economic power under the protection of the state. In particular, the newspapers played a significant role in the construction of conservative ideology in Korean society. During these regimes, there was no true competition among distinctive political viewpoints (Chae & Kim, 2008: 78). Only support for government policies was considered legitimate, and thus it monopolized Korean politics. For example, the military regimes saw "the health and security of the nation predicated on cultivating a close partnership with the United States and vigilance against the ever-menacing threat from [North Korea]" (Chae & Kim, 2008: 77). Any efforts to introduce ideological elements into the political process that were viewed as left-wing were suppressed by the state "that feared North Korean infiltration and influence, as well as their own loss of power" (Steinberg & Shin, 2006: 521). The military regimes continuously used the existence of North Korea as an excuse for their authoritarian rule. Those who attempted to introduce social reform were harshly dealt with under the Anti-Communist Act and the National Security Act (K. Cho, 1997; Kraft, 2008),[1] and the news media reported this government's suppressive treatments as an inevitable result to maintain national security (Yoon, 2010: 260).

---

1 The Anti-Communist Act (Law No. 643 of 1961) and the National Security Act (Law No. 549 of 1960) were repealed and replaced in 1980 by a new law, also named the National Security Act (Law No. 3318, December 31, 1980), which incorporated most of the Anti-Communist Act (Yoon, 2010).

These meanings and values have become the basis of the Korean conservative forces' agenda and prevailed in Korean society. Consequently, the political discourse that the news media produced in this period became the ideological ground of conservatism in Korean society.

In addition, while many journalists who played watchdog were forced to quit their jobs, the other journalists who did not play watchdog enjoyed their privileges provided by the authoritarian government. In particular, several former journalists of the news organizations played a significant role in the military regimes, and this allowed the news organizations to become another political power. Many former journalists served as government officials, such as press secretaries (Kang, 2002). These positions were often given to the journalists as rewards for cooperating with the military regimes. The media companies also welcomed the recruitment of their employees to the government because they could provide a direct connection to politicians and officials who may have had high-class information (Park et al., 2000: 114). For example, Huh Moon-Do, a former *Chosun Ilbo* reporter, became the Chun regime's chief secretary and was "the driving force behind the merging and abolition of the media industry in 1980" (Kang, 2002). A network of power was formed through "these journalist-turned-politicians or bureaucrats, which functioned effectively during periods when there was a transition of power such as during presidential elections" (Park et al., 2000: 114–115).

Ironically enough, the government's media suppression also allowed certain media companies to expand their businesses. During these military regimes, the media companies began to acquire the features of an industry, and it was subordinate to political power (Park et al., 2000: 113). In the 1960s, Park's regime cancelled the license of several media companies for political reasons (J. U. Kim, 2000), and this led to oligopolistic market structures in the media industry. A few newspapers used the forced closure of many media companies as opportunities for rapid growth (Park et al., 2000: 114). In particular, the three mainstream conservative newspapers—the *Chosun Ilbo*, the *JoongAng Ilbo*, and the *Dong-A Ilbo* (known as the "big three" papers or "*Cho-Joong-Dong*" in Korea)—monopolized the revenue from the advertising market, which was rapidly expanding with the growth of the national economy (J. U. Kim, 2000).

Collusive Relationships among the Media, Business Imperatives, and Political Power after the Transition to Democracy in Korea

During the two military regimes, Korean progressive groups were continuously challenging the authority and legitimacy of the government. Particularly, student groups, labor unions, religious organizations, and progressive intellectuals played main roles in forming the Minjung Movement in the 1970s and 1980s (S. Kim, 2000: 50–76). *Minjung* means "common people" as opposed to elites and leaders. Minjung came to "signify those who are oppressed in the sociopolitical system but who are capable of rising up against it" (Lee, 2007: 5). The progressive intellectuals and student activists of the Minjung Movement attempted to redefine the role of common people and the nature of their community. These new historical interpretations were then "deployed into the public arena through various public forums, seminars, commemoration services, and protests" (Lee, 2007: 6). The Minjung Movement not only provided the foundation of the progressivism in Korea, but also became the driving force for the country's transition from the military regime to the parliamentary democracy in 1987.

In June 1987, Korean citizens' pro-democratic efforts finally led to the breakdown of the military regime. In that year, students, the opposing party, and citizen groups of civil society forged an alliance and mobilized to demand direct presidential voting (Chang, 2005: 927). As the military yielded to their demand, Korea was undergoing a transition to democracy. As a result, direct control over the media by the government through censorship, manipulation and other measures was decreased. The new 1987 Constitution explicitly prohibits censorship of speech and the press while guaranteeing freedom of expression. The Basic Press Act of 1980 was abolished in November 1980 and replaced by the Act Relating to Registration of Periodicals (Periodicals Act) and the Broadcasting Act.

Nonetheless, the chance of transmitting alternative voices from civil society to the political system was still not guaranteed. Although authoritarian rule broke down, the conservatives maintained power in Korean society. President Roh Tae-Woo, who was elected in the first presidential election under the new 1987 Constitution, was the leader of the then-ruling conservative party. Roh was a close comrade of Dictator Chun Doo-Hwan since their days in the military academy. Roh was also "designated as Chun's successor by Chun himself" (Yoon, 2010: 32). The mainstream media supported the Roh government through producing even more conservative discourses to keep their power and property (Chang, 2005: 927–928). In the news coverage in the mainstream media, disagreement with the Roh government's policies was described as "signs of faltering [democracy] because of resistance from vested interest groups that managed to transform themselves and survive in the era of democracy" (Chang, 2005: 927–928).

Furthermore, rapid economic growth expanded the power of *chaebol*s and allowed them to gain an influence on the media system. *Chaebol* refers to South Korean conglomerates of several companies clustered around one parent company. These companies hold shares in each other and are usually managed by one single family based on authoritarian management and centralized decision making. Since the rule of the two authoritarian regimes, chaebols have given political funds to the government "in exchange for monopolistic business privileges" (Jo & Kim, 2004: 295). Chaebols have utilized public relations to avoid negative criticism of their close relations with the government and business malpractices; in-house public relations departments have attempted to maintain regular communication channels with the news media to avoid unfavorable coverage (D. Cho, 1997: 67–75). Furthermore, some chaebols run their own media firms, and others use their power over the news media through the provision of advertisement revenues (Park et al., 2000: 116).

The collusive relationships among the mainstream conservative newspapers and chaebols have been significantly reinforced since 1988 when President Roh Tae-Woo eased regulations on the establishment of periodicals. Although the number of dailies increased from twenty-eight in 1987 to sixty-five in 1988, the competition among the media companies failed to create diverse voices in media discourse (Park et al., 2000: 116). Rather, the increased number of the media companies facilitated more competition for gaining profits through advertisements. In particular, the existing news-papers, which had enjoyed monopolies on the media industry during the military regimes, decided to liberalize subscription fees and increase the number of pages to obtain more advertisements. They often delivered news-papers to readers free of charge to boost their circulation. These aspects of unfair rivalry guaranteed the established papers secure advertising revenue but made it difficult for newcomers to enter the market (Park et al., 2000: 117).

Particularly, the big three conservative papers—the *Chosun Ilbo*, the *JoongAng Ilbo*, and the *Dong-A Ilbo*—have joined the rank of chaebols through strategic marriages with chaebols' families. There are direct or indirect marital relationships among the big three papers and the 30 top chabols in Korea (G. M. Cho, 2005). Since that time, the big three papers and chaebols have been considered a collective actor "with closely aligned interests and well coordinated strategies, capable of acting concertedly as one" (Han, 2008: 2). The conservative dominance in the Korean media sys-tem, based on the close relationships with the political establishment and capital, has continuously led to a deep-seated dysfunction, as evidenced in the lack of journalistic ethics, distorted news reporting, and dependence on private relations.

Grassroots Efforts to Foster Diversity in Media Discourse in the 1970s and 1980s

During the period of authoritarian dictatorship and domesticated media between the 1970s and 1980s, the Korean citizens did not remain passive recipients of the news media. Since that time, the oligopoly of the media market and the collusion among the political power, capital, and media owners have contributed to "the growing alienation of the audiences" and consequently to "the rise of the public outcry for more freedom of the press and democratic broadcasting" (Kim, 2001: 94). Many journalists have continued to struggle to achieve the right to freedom of opinion and expression, and the audiences supported the journalists' resistance and conducted a campaign against the government's media control. A crucial example is the incident at the *Dong-A Ilbo* in 1974-5, which led to the dismissal of 134 journalists.

In October 1974, journalists of the *Dong-A Ilbo* adopted the Declaration on Practicing Freedom of the Press, in which they rejected "outside intervention in press organizations and protested the illegal arrests of journalists by the authorities" (Park et al., 2000: 118). Many groups of Korean citizens —such as college students, clergy, writers, and professors—supported the declaration and followed it. However, the authoritarian government did not allow it. The government forced the advertisers to discontinue advertising for the *Dong-A Ilbo* and its two sister media firms, the monthly *Shin Dong-A* and the *Dong-A Broadcasting System* (DBS). Although countless citizens supported the *Dong-A Ilbo* company by placing personal advertisements in the media, the company could not endure its financial difficulties caused by the advertisers' boycott. The *Dong-A Ilbo* finally surrendered to the demands of the authoritarian regime by firing all of the journalists who signed the Declaration on Practicing Freedom of the Press and turned its stance to pro-government. This incident, however, confirmed the existence of a group of active citizens, "who [fought], in various ways, against the politico-economic power oppressing the freedom of the press and against the abusive media power itself" (Park et al., 2000: 118).

This grassroots power increased the organized *media activism* in the late 1980s. Korean citizens' media activism in the early 1980s particularly focused on the campaigns for a critical understanding of the broadcasting media, which was totally controlled by the authoritarian government. These campaigns were led by Christian and Catholic churches and some civic groups; they attempted to educate the citizens and consequently contributed to the increase of public awareness of the problem. This movement provided the basis for a boycott movement against the *Korean Broadcasting System* (*KBS*) in the late 1980s (Young-Han Kim, 2001: 95-97).

In addition, during the 1970s and the 1980s, civic groups and religious groups produced and circulated a diverse form of alternative media.[2] The alternative media—including books, leaflets, discs, and videotapes—were produced without official permits. For example, in 1986, the National Council of Churches (NCC) handed out 50,000 adhesive labels and 10,000 leaflets to people, which said, 'WE DO NOT WATCH THE *KBS-TV*' (Young-Han Kim, 2001: 96). These illegal publications functioned as a catalyst for the development of the boycott movement against the *KBSTV* reception fee. This boycott movement "not only succeeded in changing the *KBS* policy on subscription fees and advertisements, but also contributed to the formation of solidarity among the grassroots movements during the nationwide democratization movement in June 1987" (Park et al., 2000: 119).[3]

Since the democratization movement in June 1987, diversity in media discourse has arisen, though in a limited degree, as new alternative media companies attempted to break up the existing conservative oligopoly in the media system. The most significant incident was the establishment of *The Hankyoreh*. *The Hankyoreh* was founded in May 1988 mostly by journalists dismissed from the *Chosun Ilbo* and the *Dong-A Ilbo* for political reasons during the military regimes in the 1970s and the 1980s. *The Hankyoreh* was intended to provide an independent, left-leaning, and nationalist alternative to mainstream conservative newspapers. The money needed to start *The Hankyoreh* was collected from approximately 62,000 citizens, and they still own *The Hankyoreh* as shareholders. Along with the foundation of *The Hankyoreh*, several relatively small alternative media companies, such as *Media Today* published by the Association of Media Labor Unions, have also emerged. These alternative media companies have continued to function as

2 In the Korean context, the term "alternative" has two meanings: first, an attempt by the new media to replace the existing media; second, a more proactive attempt to reform society by constructing counter-arguments that negate the mainstream order.

3 As a state-owned "public corporation," the *KBS* has been financed by paid advertisement, in addition to a "reception fee," i.e. a mandatory monthly viewing fee from the viewers. For more details about the boycott campaign against the *KBS* in the 1980s and its role in democratization in Korea, see Young-Han Kim (2001).

"a spokesman for progressive groups" (Park et al., 2000: 120).

FROM TOP-DOWN PRESSURES TO GRASSROOTS EFFORTS FOR MEDIA REFORM DURING TWO LIBERAL-PROGRESSIVE ADMINISTRATIONS

The Korean Financial Crisis and its Influence on the Media System in the Late 1990s

Following the Roh Tae-Woo administration, Kim Young-Sam was elected to 14th President in 1992. Kim Young-Sam enjoyed much more legitimacy than his predecessor Roh Tae-Woo, since he had no association with the military dictatorship. Hence, Kim named his government Korea's first *civilian government*, drawing "a distinction from the previous government although he was elected from the same [conservative] party" (Yoon, 2010: 34).

The Kim Young-Sam administration rapidly changed outdated practices prevailing in Korean society. In particular, to acquire memberships in the World Trade Organization (WTO) in 1995 and the Organization for Economic Cooperation and Development (OECD) in 1996, the Kim Young-Sam administration reformed relevant laws and regulations to fulfill global standards, resulting in financial liberalization and economic deregulation. This rapid reform of the financial system caused an unprecedented economic crisis represented by the International Monetary Fund (IMF) bailout in 1997 (Yoon, 2010: 34–37).

In spite of several precursors of the economic crisis, the Kim Young-Sam government continued to announce that the foundation of the Korean economy was still strong as late as mid-1997. The mainstream media also supported the government's economic policies by downplaying the seriousness of the financial crisis. According to Shim (2002), the mainstream conservative newspapers were, in part, responsible for the economic crisis in the late 1990s as they misled the Korean public by "[continuously painting a rosy picture] about the prospects of the Korean economy" (Shim, 2002: 345).

The economic crisis for which the Kim Young-Sam administration was responsible helped opposition candidate Kim Dae-Jung to prevail in the 1997 presidential election. The success of Kim Dae-Jung was "another boost of momentum for the development of Korea's democracy" (Yoon, 2010: 38). For the first time in modern Korean history, peaceful transfer of political power from the ruling conservative party to the opposition progressive party took place; it was 10 years after the beginning of transition to democracy in 1987.

Although the IMF bailout package imposed enormous difficulties on the country, the new progressive government took advantage from these difficulties to make a fundamental reform in the financial system and business practices and other related areas. The crisis consequently contributed to enhancing transparency particularly in the business system (Yoon, 2010: 37–39). The Kim Dae-Jung government also adopted the policy for socio-economic restructuring, saying "it is the only way for the country to survive" (Park et al., 2000: 122).

Many Korean media companies also faced a challenge for their ownership structure in the restructuring process. Several daily newspapers separated from their mother business groups (i.e., chaebols). In 1998, the *Kyanghyang Shinmun*, the *JoongAng Ilbo*, and the *Munhwa Ilbo* separated from Hanwha, Samsung and Hyundai groups, respectively. Particularly, after its separation from Hanwha group, the *Kyunghyang Shinmun* changed its ownership structure into the employee-ownership.[4] Since that time, all employees, including 240 journalists, have comprised the biggest shareholders of the *Kyunghyang*

4 The *Munhwa Ilbo* is owned by the Moon-Woo Foundation for Journalism and the Dong-yang Foundation for Culture, which have a total of 61.3% of the company's stocks. These two foundations were established by Hyundai Heavy Industries. The *JoongAng Ilbo* is owned by the Hong family (44% of the company's stocks) and CJ Corporation (21%). CJ Corporation was originally part of Samsung group, but separated in 1995. Nonetheless, the two chaebols still keep very close ties to this day. The president of CJ Corporation is the grandson of the former president of Samsung group, Lee Byung-Chull. Many critics have argued that these ownerships may still influence the news reporting of the *Munhwa Ilbo* and the *JoongAng Ilbo* (e.g., S.-S. Kim, 2002).

Shinmun, and the rest has been owned by retired employees and the company (*Kyunghyang Shinmun*, 2005). This separation has led the *Kyunghyang Shinmun* to be more critical of the conservative forces and chaebols.[5]

The Media Tax Audit during Kim Dae-Jung's Presidency

The Kim Dae-Jung government had an extremely tense relationship with the big three conservative newspapers. In 2001, the Kim Dae-Jung government audited possible violations of tax and fair trade laws among a total of twenty-three media companies. As a result, the National Tax Service and the Fair Trade Commission assessed a total of $388 million in back taxes and penalties against the big three papers (Kirk, 2001b). Consequently, Bang Sang-Hoon (president and owner of the *Chosun Ilbo*) and Kim Byung-Kwan (principal owner and honorary chairman of the *Dong-A Ilbo*) went to prison for tax evasion, and An Kyung-Hee (the wife of Kim Byung-Kwan) committed suicide during the investigation.[6] At the same time, the Fair Trade Commission composed a list of several violations of the fair trade act by the big three papers and imposed penalties. The list included "the printing of hundreds of thousands of extra copies as a way to inflate circulation figures and raise advertising prices, forcing newsdealers to take more copies than they [could] sell and asking suppliers of newsprint to donate gifts for company-sponsored events" (Kirk, 2001a). The tax audit seriously damaged the reputation of the big three conservative newspapers (Shin, 2005: 30).

The Kim Dae-Jung government denied any relationship between the tax

5 According to its mission statement (*Kyunghyang Shinmun*, 2005), the *Kyunghyang Shinmun* "support[s] the moderate progressive in which [the *Kyunghyang Shinmun*] champion[s] the cause of a better life for the ordinary people since the South Korean government spends less than 8% of its GDP for its social security network. [The *Kyunghyang Shinmun*] support[s] economic policies in favor of small and medium businesses and the Sunshine Policy of engagement with North Korea."

6 As a precedent in 1999, Hong Seok-Hyun (president and owner of the *JoongAng Ilbo*) was also put in jail for two months, "fined $2.65 million and ordered to pay $9 million in back taxes on charges of having evaded taxes against a separate company he [controlled] with other family members" (Kirk, 2001a).

investigation and the President's intention of reforming the media; however, the conservatives argued that the tax audit was nothing but a severe violation of press freedom (Kirk, 2001b). The then-majority conservative Grand National Party and the big three conservative newspapers contended that the government's motivation behind the tax investigation was to suppress the papers' criticism against Kim Dae-Jung and his policies. While Kim Dae-Jung carried out new policies that favored the middle—and lower—income classes by enacting new laws and changing previous ones (Yoon, 2010: 38), the conservative forces were repeatedly criticizing almost every government policies. In particular, the big three papers showed an extremely negative view towards the government foreign policy towards North Korea.[7] They contended that the tax audit was an attempt to regulate the media as revenge for such criticism.

The 386 Generation, the Internet, and the 2002 Presidential Election

Following Kim Dae-Jung, Roh Moo-Hyun was successful in the 2002 presidential election. The 2002 presidential election is one of the most significant events in Korean democracy. In early 2002, Roh Moo-Hyun was nominated by the liberal-progressive Millennium Democratic Party through primary elections. For the first time in Korean political history, these primaries enabled ordinary party members to choose a presidential candidate (Yoon, 2010: 39–40). This political event successfully attracted public attention.[8]

In December 2002, Roh Moo-Hyun defeated Lee Hoi-Chang of the opposition conservative Grand National Party in the presidential election.

---

7 The Kim Dae-Jung government's foreign policy towards North Korea is referred to *Sunshine Policy*. This policy broke away from past policies as it aimed at "engaging rather than confronting North Korea through dialogue, exchange, and cooperation" (Yoon, 2010: 38). In 2000, Kim Dae-Jung was awarded the Nobel Peace Prize as a result of Sunshine Policy.

8 As a reaction, the conservative Grand National Party also conducted the primary system but failed to draw broad public attention (Yoon, 2010: 40).

This result surprised the nation because most presidential campaign polls had shown Roh Moo-Hyun falling behind Lee Hoi-Chang (Jinsun Lee, 2009: 25–26). These two major candidates had "diametrically opposing characteristics, not only in ideological and political stances, but also in personal and family backgrounds" (Shin, 2005: 27–28). Roh Moo-Hyun was born in a poor farming family. He taught himself law and passed the bar examination in 1975. As a human rights lawyer and an advocate for laborers and activists, Roh Moo-Hyun defended college students and activists who were arrested during the pro-democratic movement, such as the Minjung Movement, in the 1970s and 1980s (Jinsun Lee, 2009; Yoon, 2010). On the other hand, Lee Hoi-Chang was born and raised in an elite family; his father was a public prosecutor. Lee studied law at Seoul National University and became a judge at the age of twenty-five. Lee had a very successful legal career as a judge and became the country's youngest-ever chief judge of the Constitutional Court (Shin, 2005). During the Kim Young-Sam administration, Lee Hoi-Chang was the Prime Minister, as well as the head of the conservative Grand National Party. Due to these different careers and histories between the two candidates, the victory of Roh Moo-Hyun was "an unpredictable political drama that people had never experienced" (Yoon, 2010: 40).

The election of Roh was even more stunning in light of the fact that the mainstream conservative media fully supported the conservative candidate, Lee Hoi-Chang, during the entire process of the presidential campaign. The big three conservative newspapers (i.e., the *Chosun Ilbo*, the *JoongAng Ilbo*, and the *Dong-A Ilbo*) severely condemned Roh's campaign promises (K. Lee, 2003). Korean scholars and critics believed that the big three papers, which dominated the Korean newspaper market with a combined readership of 75–80 percent in 2002, played a crucial role in agenda-setting during the presidential campaign (Kim & Johnson, 2006; Jinsun Lee, 2009). The liberal-progressive groups sarcastically called the big three papers "kingmakers in presidential elections" (K. Lee, 2005: 11). Roh's victory in the 2002 presidential election therefore served as a warning of the changing landscape of media power in Korea, particularly to the mainstream conservative newspapers.

No one would dispute that Roh owed his victory to the liberal-progressive young voters. Many scholars and critics emphasize the impact of the online activities of the liberal-progressives in their twenties and thirties during the presidential campaign (e.g., Kim & Johnson, 2006; Jinsun Lee, 2009). After the presidential election in December 2002, many foreign news media also ran headlines such as "The World's First Internet President Logs On" (The Guardian, 2003) and "Online Newspaper Shakes up Korean Politics" (The New York Times, 2003).

The role of one group, *NOSAMO*, which is a Korean acronym for "People Who Love Roh Moo-Hyun," was particularly prominent during the entire process of the presidential campaign. NOSAMO was an online-based political *fan club* that supported Roh as a politician and a candidate in the primaries of the Millennium Democratic Party and presidential campaign. The members of NOSAMO were mostly those Koreans in their twenties, thirties, and forties with liberal-progressive political orientations. The members of NOSAMO effectively informed the public through the Internet about Roh Moo-Hyun's campaign promises, such as support for the Sunshine Policy toward North Korea and *chaebol* reform. The members of NOSAMO argued that the big three conservative papers misinformed the public through biased reporting and distortion of facts (Shin, 2005: 38). The members used the Internet as their outlet where they could communicate with each other and create "a counteragenda forum against the conservative papers" (Rhee, 2003). Particularly, NOSAMO treated online alternative newspapers, such as the *OhmyNews* and the *Seoprise*, as the outlets that provided a reliable source of news. NOSAMO spread the information via its homepage (www.nosamo.org), bulletin board systems (BBS) of the online media, and web messengers (Jinsun Lee, 2009: 26).

Among the members, *the 386 generation* led the NOSAMO's activities during the entire process of the presidential campaign (Kim & Hamilton, 2006: 554). Coined in the 1990s, *the 386 generation* refers to those who were in their thirties, entered the universities in the 1980s, and were born in the 1960s. The 386 generation had played a crucial role as the force of student power in the Minjung Movement in the 1980s and the June Democracy Movement that terminated decades of two military regimes in 1987 (Kim & Hamilton, 2006: 553). Members of the 386 generation have been more skeptical of the United States compared with the older generations. This is largely because the U.S. had "backed the same military regimes they had fought against" (Fairclough, 2004).[9] Growing into their forties by the 2000s, they began to hold important positions in politics and business.

NOSAMO's success in the 2002 presidential campaign was the result of the long-term process of the appropriation and strategic use of the Internet for social change by the 386 generation. As Clay Shirky (2008) writes, the Internet "[did] not know what it [would be] used for" when it first emerged (Shirky, 2008: 157). Considering the social and political conditions of Korea's recent history, it seems only natural that reform-oriented liberal-progressives would actively appropriate online media to produce and share their opinions and to participate in political actions. Before the 2002 presidential election, the liberal-progressive appropriation of the Internet underwent three phases of development in Korea.

The three phases of the liberal-progressive appropriation of the Internet between the late 1980s and early 2000s

In the first phase, between the late 1980s and early 1990s, the 386 generation, particularly college students and liberal-progressive white-collar workers, began to construct online communities. These online communities became the *pioneers* of creating Korean web culture. In this period, "386" was the name of the latest Central Processing Unit (CPU) model, the Intel 80386 or i386, developed by Intel. The 386 generation thus also referred to "early adopters of new media technology" in Korea (Jinsun Lee, 2009: 123–124). Between 1985 and 1994, three telecommunication companies— *Chollian*, *Hitel* (formerly, *Ketel*), and *Naunuri*—first launched their bulletin

---

9 The influence of the 386 generation can be "comparable to that of the baby boomers in the U.S., many of whose political views were shaped by anti-Vietnam War protests and the civil-rights movement" (Fairclough, 2004).

board systems (BBS) using "PC *Tongsin*" (Personal Computer Communication), a type of data link protocol used in establishing a direct connection between two networking nodes through a phone line (Jinsun Lee, 2009: 81). Since that period, the 386 generation occupied the BBS and established several online communities based on the network servers that they mainly used and their social and political interests (Chang, 2005; Jinsun Lee, 2009).

These online communities played a pivotal role in setting the initial trend in online communication in Korea. Much jargon, which originated or was popularized by these online communities in the 1990s, is now in common use on the Internet in Korea (Jinsun Lee, 2009: 107). For example, the members of the online communities started to use an honorific suffix, *Nim*, when referring to each other regardless of age, gender, and social status. The honorific suffix, Nim, has been traditionally reserved for elders to show them respect. The usage of Nim for every member of the online communities therefore was recognized as a revolutionary action, promoting a non-hierarchical and democratic "netiquette" (net etiquette).

The second phase was characterized by the emergence of online alternative news media, such as the *Ddanzi Ilbo* (www.ddanzi.com) and the *Daejabo* (www.jabo.co.kr). In the late 1990s, these online media actively challenged the mainstream conservative media by creating, collecting, and distributing radical, alternative news, information and entertainment. One of the most significant characteristics of these online alternative media was the use of parodies in their news articles. For example, the *Ddanzi Ilbo* has published a series of parodies of the *Chosun Ilbo*, the most influential conservative daily in Korea, and these parodies were greatly popular among young liberal-progressives (Chang, 2005: 929).

In the third phase, in the early 2000s, the online alternative media led ordinary citizens to engage in the act of journalism based on the interactive and participatory form of online communication. Many communication scholars have evaluated these Korean online news media—such as, the *OhmyNews* (www.ohmynews.com), the *Issue Today* (www.issuetoday.com), and the *Pressian* (www.pressian.com)—as pioneers of "citizen journalism," which is characterized by the use of ordinary citizens as reporters, usually unpaid, in place of professional. Since their beginning, these online alternative news media have provided their own BBS and discussion forums to encourage dynamic interactions among the readers. These BBS and forums are "operated by self-regulatory rules of participants and all can freely express their opinions on the articles published" in the online media (Chang, 2005: 930).

In particular, the *OhmyNews* has been one of the most successful online news media in the world (Gillmor, 2006). The *OhmyNews* was established in February 2000 with 727 ordinary citizen reporters, but this number increased to 14,000 by October 2001 and to 20,000 by September 2002. In 2002, the majority of *OhmyNews*'s content was written by these citizen reporters, with contributions totaling more than 150 articles a day (Oh, 2004: 33). The founder of *OhmyNews*, Oh Yeon-Ho, was a former student activist as a member of the 386 generation (Gluck, 2003). In an interview with the *British Broadcasting Corporation* (*BBC*) in 2003, Oh said as follows:

> My generation, the 386 generation, were in the streets fighting in the 80s against the military dictatorship. Now, 20 years later, we are combat-ready with our Internet. . . . We really want to be part of forming public opinion—and all of us, all of the 386 generation are now deployed with the internet, ready to fight. . . . In the past, the conservative papers in Korea could—and did—lead public opinion. They had the monopoly. They were against Roh Moo-Hyun's candidacy. But *OhmyNews* supported the Roh Moo-Hyun phenomenon, with all the netizens participating. . . . In our battle between the conservative media and the netizens of Korea, the netizens won (Gluck, 2003).

From the late 1980s to early 2000s, the 386 generation was at the forefront in the process of adopting and appropriating the Internet for civic engagement. Their activities finally bore fruit in the 2002 presidential election: "Roh Moo-Hyun's victory." Since then, there has been little doubt that the online alternative news media "has edged its way into the public sphere" in Korea (Kim & Hamilton, 2006: 550). Although this does not mean that the conservative-dominated media system has been overturned, the online alternative news media have contributed to fostering diversity in the media system, combining with the influence of the existing liberal-progressive news media—such as *The Hankyoreh* and the *Kyunghyang Shinmun*—in public opinion formation. According to an annual survey that examined "the most influential media in Korea" (*Sisa Journal*, 2004), two online alternative news media (the *OhmyNews* and the *Pressian*) and one liberal-progressive newspaper (*The Hankyoreh*) entered into the top 10 media for the first time, while two major national networks (the *MBC* and the *KBS*) and the big three conservative newspapers (the *Chosun Ilbo*, the *JoongAng Ilbo*, and the *Dong-A Ilbo*) were still ranked as the top five influential media in Korea.

The Post-386 Generation and Candlelight Vigils as a Collective Action Repertoire

The post-386 generation has succeeded to the leading role of the 386 generation in conducting civic action and social resistance in Korea. Born in the 1970s and 1980s, the post-386 generation is a substantial beneficiary of the nation's rapid economic growth and democracy. Unlike the 386 genera-tion who fought against the military regimes to achieve democracy, it is only natural that the post-386 generation internalizes democratic values and rejects traditional authoritarian culture, such as the Cold War view, in all aspects of their lives. Collectively, this generation is less ideological (Kim & Hamilton, 2006: 553). They are thus simultaneously willing to criticize both the U.S. policies and North Korea's actions. In addition, the post-386 generation can be characterized by an increased use of, and familiarity with, the ICTs.

The post-386 liberal-progressives have developed a collective generational consciousness through organizing and participating in a series of political and cultural events, such as the street cheering in the 2002 Korea-Japan World Cup soccer match, the 2002 Korean Candlelight Vigil after the deaths of two middle school girls, the 2004 Korean Candlelight Vigil against the impeachment of President Roh Moo-Hyun, and ultimately, the 2008 Korean Candlelight Vigil. Through these shared experiences, the post-386 generation, particularly the young liberal-progressives, has not only enhanced existing collective action repertoires but also created new forms of online collective action and resistance in Korea. These processes of developing the means, ends, and environment of their collective actions have played a role in constructing and sustaining their collective identity.

The 2002 World Cup and the Red Devils

In May and June 2002, millions of young Koreans wearing red T-shirts gathered together in all parts of the country.[10] They collectively cheered on the streets for the Korean national soccer team. The "Red Devils," an online-based fan club for the Korean national soccer, played a pivotal role in mobilizing collective actions for the street cheering. The Red Devils started with only 200 members in 1997. However, within the one-month duration of the 2002 World Cup, more than 450,000 became new members of the Red Devils; most new members, as well as the existing members, were those in their twenties and thirties, members of the post-386 generation. They successfully informed and mobilized a massive number of massive citizens within a short period of time through the Internet (Jinsun Lee, 2009: 14– 17). The collective activities mobilized by the Red Devils redefined national- ism to include a renewed sense of national confidence and pride. Further- more, through this shared experience, the post-386 generation, which had been regarded as an extremely egocentric and politically apathetic genera- tion, emerged as a new agent of organizing collective events (Jinsun Lee, 2009).

---

10 According to Lowe-Lee (2010), 800,000 Koreans came out to the streets for Korea's match with Poland, 1,500,000 for the Korea-U.S. match and 2,800,000 for the Korea-Portugal match and 4,200,000 for Korea's quarterfinal with Italy. During the semifinal with Germany team, approximately 7,000,000 Koreans were on the streets.

The 2002 Korean Candlelight Vigil after the deaths of two middle school girls
The post-386 generation also organized the 2002 Korean Candlelight
Protest. The 2002 Korean Candlelight Protest from the deaths of two
thirteen-year-old girls. In June 13, 2002, an armored military vehicle driven
by two U.S. soldiers who were stationed in Korea ran over and killed two
Korean middle-school girls, Shim Mi-Sun and Shin Hyo-Soon (GI Korea,
2008). There was a strong desire among many Koreans that the two U.S.
soldiers should be punished. However, the Status of Forces Agreement
(SOFA) between the U.S. and Korea was applied to the U.S. soldiers' case.
The U.S. military court, not under Korean law, acquitted the two defendants
on charges of negligent homicide and described the two girls' deaths as "a
vehicular accident" (Kang, 2009: 173). However, through the Internet, the
post-386 generation defined the girls' deaths as a "national tragedy" in a
broader context of historical relationship between Korea and the U.S. and
began to severely criticize the remaining "Cold War politics and U.S. hegemony" in Korea (Kang, 2009). To show their opposition to these, the
post-386 generation protesters waged nationwide candlelight vigils.

The first candlelight vigil was initiated by one *OhmyNews*'s citizen journalist, using the name AngMA, who posted an emotional poem on the
OhmyNews's BBS.[11] A few hours after this poem was posted, it provoked a
collective response from countless Internet users. The candlelight vigil was
held on Nov. 30, 2002 with 15,000 citizens for the first time, and it continued to expand to more than 300,000 by Dec. 14, 2002. During the 2002
Korean Candlelight Protest, Korean citizens commemorated the girls'
deaths in 57 locations across the nation. Furthermore, the girls' deaths and
the renegotiation of SOFA and the Korea-U.S. relationships were the most
crucial issues in the 2002 Presidential election (Kang, 2009: 172). This political atmosphere helped build strong solidarity among young Korean liberal-
progressives, both the 386 generation and the post-386 generation, and this
was one of the driving forces underlying the election of the liberal-

11 As the AngMA's poem drew attention from the news media, he disclosed his own name
and identity: Kim, Gibo, a white-collar in his thirties (Jinsun Lee, 2009: 19).

progressive candidate Roh Moo-Hyun. Furthermore, since this time, the "candlelight vigil" has become the most popular form of collective civic action for the young Korean liberal-progressives. The young liberal-progressives have held candlelight vigils not only to commemorate memory of victims, but also to express their collective objection to various political issues.

The Impeachment of President Roh Moo-Hyun and its Influence on the 2004 General Election

President Roh Moo-Hyun wanted to reform the Korean society on the basis of *principle and common sense* "by rectifying unprincipled privilege, unreasonable practices, and irregularity by vested interest groups" (Yoon, 2010: 40–41). However, Roh had a difficult presidency from his inauguration in February 2003. The conservative then-opposition Grand National Party had the majority in the National Assembly. In addition, Roh's own party, the Millennium Democratic Party, struggled to resolve its internal conflict between those close to the previous president Kim Dae-Jung and those who identified themselves more with Roh Moo-Hyun (Lee, 2005: 409). In September 2003, the pro-Roh party members finally left the Millennium Democratic Party and established a new party, the Yeollin Uri Party. As a result, the Millennium Democratic Party turned against Roh and allied with the conservative Grand National Party. This division meant that the anti-Roh alliance formed a "supermajority" in the Assembly of 212 members out of 272 (Lee, 2005: 409). Under the Constitution of the Republic of Korea, a vote of two-thirds or more of the National Assembly is sufficient to "override the President's vetoes on legislation [(article 53)], expel members of the Assembly [(article 64)], impeach the President [(article 65)], and propose constitutional amendments to be put to national referenda [(article 130)]" (Lee, 2005: 409). Furthermore, in October 2003, some of Roh's closest aides were arrested on suspicion of accepting bribes from businesses for the Roh's 2002 presidential campaign, and these events became the targets of severe criticism.

At the peak of a political crisis with few allies in the National Assembly and rapidly decreasing job approval ratings, Roh took a series of actions to find a breakthrough (Lee, 2005). First, in October 2003, he proposed to hold a national referendum on his leadership in mid-December. Secondly, Roh agreed to resign if the amount of the bribes that his aides received during the 2002 presidential campaign exceeded one-tenth of the amount of the bribes that the opposing conservative Grand National Party received (Lee, 2005).

Third, at a press conference on February 24, 2004, President Roh openly supported the Uri Party, saying "I expect that the public will overwhelmingly support the Uri Party at the general election of April 2004," and "I would like to do anything that is legal if it may lead to votes for the Yeollin Uri Party" (Im & Kim, 2004). On February 27, 2004, the opposing parties filed a complaint to the National Election Commission, reporting that Roh violated the Election Law that prohibits any campaign activities by public officials in support of certain candidates (Im & Kim, 2004). On March 3, the National Election Commission judged that President Roh violated the Election Law and warned him to refrain from additional violations (Kim, Choi, & Cho, 2008). The opposing parties, the Grand National Party and the Millennium Democratic Party, demanded a public apology from President Roh for the violation of the Election Law and warned President Roh that he could be impeached (Lee, 2005: 411). Although Roh held a press conference and apologized to the public for the scandals that swirled around his close supporters, he refused to apologize for the violations that he made in support of the Yeollin Uri Party at the general election (Lee, 2005: 411).

On March 12, the opposing parties finally passed a motion to impeach President Roh. Among 212 lawmakers of the opposing parties in the National Assembly, 193 voted for the impeachment and two voted against it, while all forty-seven Yeollin Uri Party lawmakers refused to participate in it (Kim, Choi, & Cho, 2008). Based on the Constitution, Roh's presidency was immediately suspended, and the Prime Minster, Goh Kun, took over the duties of the President (Lee, 2005: 412).

The impeachment of Roh Moo-Hyun caused a huge public dissent in Korea, with several polls showing that 70 percent of Korean citizens opposed the impeachment. According to the Constitution, the Constitutional Court was "the institution that had the responsibility to resolve this political dispute" (Lee, 2005: 412). As the Constitutional Court deliberated, the impeachment vote became the most crucial campaign issue in the upcoming general election in April 2004.

Korean citizens held candlelight vigils across the country to protest the impeachment, and the 386 and post-386 liberal-progressives led these vigils (Fairclough, 2004). Between March 12 and 29, a cumulative 1.5 million Koreans (approximately 3.1 percent of all Koreans) participated in the candlelight vigils (Jung, 2008: 19). Korean citizens demanded that the National Assembly nullify the impeachment and call for an apology from the opposing parties for their decision.

In addition, young Korean liberal-progressives actively supported the "defeat movement" being held by the Citizens' Alliance for the 2004 General Election (CAGE). The CAGE was organized with more than 290 civic organizations to provide a list of candidates who were considered unfit to be elected. On April 6, 2004, the CAGE published a blacklist of 208 politicians who were targeted for defeat in the 2004 general election, including 139 lawmakers who had voted for the impeachment of President Roh. Following the CAGE, 193 student organizations also formed the College Students' Alliance for the 2004 General Election and conducted their own campaigns to vote against the blacklisted politicians.

The 2004 general election was held on April 15. The liberal-progressive party, Yeollin Uri Party, became the majority of the National Assembly for the first time in Korean history with 152 out of the 299 Assembly seats, while the conservative Grand National Party won 121 seats. The progressive Democratic Labor Party, whose support base was mainly laborers and farmers, also emerged as the third-largest party in the National Assembly. On the contrary, the Millennium Democratic Party, which had been the second-largest party prior to the 2004 general election, "ended up with mere nine seats" in the backlash following its leading role in the impeachment of

Roh (Lee, 2005: 412).

After the 2004 general election, on May 14, the Constitutional Court announced its judgment rejecting the National Assembly's motion of the impeachment and reinstating Roh Moo-Hyun. President Roh thereby returned to his office sixty-three days after suspension of presidential authority (Lee, 2005: 414). This decision mostly received positive response throughout the country; according to a poll, approximately 84 percent of Korean citizens reported that they agreed with the Constitutional Court's decision (Im & Yi, 2004).

The Roh Moo-Hyun Government's Effort to Reform the Media System

After the victory of his liberal-progressive Yeollin Uri Party in the 2004 general election, President Roh was able to carry out his progressive platform more actively. A large number of elected lawmakers were part of the 386 generation, and more than ten were former presidents and officers of the nationwide organization, National Committee of University Student Representatives, that had led the pro-democratic movement in the 1980s (Lee, 2007: 301–302).[12] During their four-year term, the liberal-progressive lawmakers were more nationalistic, more humanitarian, more accommodating toward North Korea, and more skeptical about American-oriented policies.

President Roh directly targeted the Korean press as an institution that he intended to reform. First of all, Roh gave government officials a "not-to-do" list to terminate the old practices between government and press in Korea. For example, Roh ordered that no officials were to subscribe to the "street editions" of the daily newspapers.[13] In previous governments, officials "hunted for unfavorable news coverage in street editions and then contacted editors to tell them not to carry such reporting in the morning edition" (K.

---

12 Many 386 generation lawmakers in the National Assembly also have belonged to the conservative Grand National Party, whose leaders would have been the protest targets in the 1980s (N. Lee, 2007: 302).

13 In Korea, morning newspapers are available as "street editions" on the previous evening.

Lee, 2003). Under the new policy, when a government official found any error in news coverage of the government, challenging the error had to be done "by legal channels, not by negotiating with reporters or editors or doing anything illegal" (K. Lee, 2003). In addition, Roh advised the officials not to provide any favors to journalists and editors so that friendly reports would be written. Cabinet members and government officials were told not to dine or drink with reporters; President Roh argued that in doing this, the government made the press a powerhouse without responsibility.

The Roh government and the then-ruling liberal-progressive Yeollin Uri Party also attempted to re-distribute media power and foster diversity in media discourse through enacting related laws. The parliament passed two media related laws in 2005: the Newspaper Law and the Press Arbitration Law. These laws emphasized "the social responsibilities of the media to the general public and respect pluralism" (Sa, 2009a: 11). Particularly, these laws aimed to stop the mainstream newspapers from engaging in unfair competition in the newspaper industry (Sa, 2009b).[14] However, the mainstream newspapers filed a petition to the Constitutional Court of Korea, describing the laws as too strict compared to those applied to non-newspaper companies. In 2006, the court ruled that some articles of the laws were unconstitutional, saying the articles were contrary to press freedom and business freedom in that they limited the market share a newspaper could obtain.

Roh Moo-Hyun continuously struggled to deal with the mainstream conservative newspapers, particularly the big three papers. These conservative newspapers criticized most of Roh's policies. This struggle already existed since the previous liberal-progressive government. During the tax audit of the media companies during previous Kim Dae-Jung government, Roh condemned the big three papers publicly and argued for "payment of taxes as the rightful cost of doing business" (K. Lee, 2003). During his

14 The Newspaper Law was a revision of the existing law on the Registration of Periodicals. The Press Arbitration Law combines features of two existing laws—the Act Relating to Registration of Periodicals (Periodicals Act) and the Broadcasting Act—into a single law, dealing with press arbitration and damage relief (Sa, 2009a: 11).

presidency, Roh claimed that since the conservative newspapers had strayed from reporting fairly, government officials should continue to "engage in controversies" with the newspapers and this interfered with the officials' works. The Roh governmental bodies made a total of 752 legal claims against the press, a significantly higher number of lawsuits than any preceding government. In August 2003, President Roh also filed a $2.5 million lawsuit against four newspapers, including the big three papers, and one opposition lawmaker "for their report that a charge of speculative real estate trading had been brought against him" (K. Lee, 2003). In the lawsuit, Roh Moo-Hyun accused the papers of comprehensive, persistent, and massive defamation of my character that, not as president but as a human being, caused me psychological agony hard to express in words. Although Roh agreed to postpone legal action until finishing his term as President, this lawsuit was the first legal claim against the press made by the President of Korea.

Despite the attempts to remake the media system during the two liberal-progressive governments, the Kim Dae-Jung government and the Roh Moo-Hyun government, the reform of the news media was difficult to accomplish. The majority of news organizations was still seen as part of the conservative sphere and supported the vested interests of the conservative forces. The public opinion about media reform was also mixed. Since the 2002 presidential election, the generation gap in political orientation has been wider and so it has been in media reform issue. An understanding of the need for media reform was increasing among the younger generation; however, the majority of those Koreans born in the 1930s and 1940s strongly supported the conservative party and read the big three conservative newspapers. In addition, many Koreans did not want media reform to come from the government, fearing that would damage democracy (Sa, 2009a). The mainstream conservative media regarded the topdown pressures for media reform as attempts to regulate the media, and the word "media regulation" often recalled the military regimes and their media control of Korean people's minds (K. Lee, 2003). Additionally, international organizations separated into opposing sides regarding the role of government in reforming the media system in Korea. For example, while the International Press Institute and the World Association of Newspapers responded negatively to the tax audit of media companies in 2001, the International Federation of Journalists responded positively to it (Sa, 2009a).

THE RETURN TO CONSERVATIVE RULE IN KOREA
AND THE EMERGENCE OF THE 2008 KOREAN CANDLELIGHT VIGIL

In the December 2007 presidential election, the conservative candidate Lee Myung-Bak won the election by a clear majority, beating the rival liberal-progressive candidates on a campaign promising economic growth. During the campaign, Lee Myung-Bak spoke strongly to the public dissatisfaction with the tenure of President Roh Moo-Hyun in which "economic inequality had continued to widen and [become] irregular, casual and temporary forms of work expand" (Doucette, 2010: 23). The conservative Grand National Party and Lee Myung-Bak described the decade of liberal-progressive rule by the Kim Dae-Jung government and the Roh Moo-Hyun government as the *lost decade* of diminished economic growth (Doucette, 2010; Paik, 2007). While the conservative forces effectively constructed clear images of the lost decade through the news frame of the mainstream conservative newspapers and newly-established online conservative news media, the Korean liberal-progressive bloc split into several factions (Paik, 2007).

The split of the liberal-progressive group was largely caused by the policy choices of the Roh Moo-Hyun government. Although Roh began his tenure with ambitious reform plans, he suffered "defeat in most of [his] policy areas" (Doucette, 2010: 34). In particular, the decision to dispatch troops to Iraq and the failure of reforms in the labor market and the media system led to tensions between President Roh and the ruling liberal-progressive Yeollin Uri Party, as well as between his government and civil society groups. Many Korean liberal-progressives felt betrayed by Roh Moo-Hyun because his government seemed to reverse its economic philosophy from progressivism to neo-liberalism.[15] The Roh Moo-Hyun government attempted to privatize public sectors and negotiate a free trade agreement with the United States, while it failed to carry out substantial reform of real estate and education policy (Choi, 2007). By the end of Roh's tenure, several liberal-progressive party members and government officials who advocated progressive economic reform resigned and publicly criticized the Roh Moo-Hyun administration (Doucette, 2010: 35).

During the 2007 presidential campaign, the conservative camp chose to fight the election on the economic issue and successfully used the Internet to inform the public. After the success of the online campaign of Roh Moo-Hyun in the 2002 presidential election, the mainstream media began to aggressively adopt the ICTs. In particular, the big three conservative papers —the *Chosun Ilbo*, the *JoongAng Ilbo*, and the *Dong-A Ilbo*—established *the department of online news* and started to provide the BBS on their online news websites (Jinsun Lee, 2009: 103). In addition, several conservative online news media, such as the *Newdaily* and the *Dailian*, were also established in the mid 2000s. These conservative news media fully supported the conservative candidate, Lee Myung-Bak, during the entire process of the 2007 presidential campaign.

On the contrary, the influence of the online alternative news media, such as the *OhmyNews* and the *Pressian*, on public opinion formation in the 2007 presidential election was relatively decreased compared to the 2002 presidential election. Between 2002 and 2007, every year the number of Koreans who described themselves as regular visitors of the online alternative news media continued to fall. This is largely because most Internet users have got their news directly from major portal sites, such as *NAVER* and *DAUM*, since the portals launched their own newsgathering system between 2002 and 2003. Most press publishers have competitively sold news articles "to the portals as much as they could sell the one-source multi-use articles" (Jang, 2006: 185). Since then, Korean Internet users have had free access to almost every news article of any news media, and consequently, the online

---

15 Neo-liberal economic policies can be characterized by emphasizing economic efficiency and advocating economic liberalization, free trade, and open markets (Doucette, 2010).

alternative news media have faced financial difficulties. The online alternative news media have been losing not only their advertising revenue, but also their influence on public opinion formation, to portal sites.[16]

During the election campaign, Lee Myung-Bak emphasized that his government would move from the age of ideology into the age of pragmatism. However, soon after Lee's election, it seemed that he had been making false promises. Even the conservative US-based think-tank, the Heritage Foundation, evaluated Lee Myung-Bak as "a conservative candidate with an ideological mandate." The institution also argued that "his pragmatism [was] simply a rhetorical attempt to avoid association with the old guard in the [conservative Grand National Party] in order to attract younger voters" (Doucette, 2010: 23).

As soon as Lee Myung-Bak started his term as the President in 2008, Lee and this conservative party severely condemned the two previous liberal-progressive governments. In their conservative views, the successive liberal-progressive rule had strained a close Korea-US relationship, endangered national security by pursuing the Sunshine Policy toward North Korea, and overlooked economic development by attempting to reform the chaebols.

The Lee government announced that they were going to abolish the legacy of the *lost decade*, starting with consolidation of the Korea-USA relationship. On April 18 2008, the Lee government agreed with the U.S. government to lift the import ban on U.S. beef. This agreement, viewed by many Koreans to be a signal of an unfair deal, caused the 2008 Korean Candlelight Vigil. Within his first few months in office, Lee's approval ratings dropped faster than any predecessors, and top government officials and ministers subsequently resigned (Doucette, 2010: 24–25).

16 In the 2008 annual survey by the Korea Press Foundation, the big three conservative papers and three portal sites were ranked in the top 10 influential media, but no online alternative news media was included (Oh, 2008).

U.S. Beef Imports in Korea before the 2008 Korean Candlelight Vigil

Korea was the third largest export market for U.S. beef until the Korean government banned U.S. beef imports when bovine spongiform encephalopathy (BSE, more commonly known as Mad Cow Disease) was first reported in the United States in December 2003. When President Roh Moo-Hyun expressed his intention to negotiate a free trade agreement with the U.S. in 2005, several officials of the U.S. government made clear that their support of the free trade agreement depended on whether or not the Korean government resumed the U.S. beef imports (Shin, 2009: 568–569).

Shortly before the two governments announced their intent to negotiate the free trade agreement in February 2006, the Roh Moo-Hyun government agreed to a partial lifting of the import ban on U.S. beef. The Roh government would allow "the importation of boneless U.S. beef derived from cattle less than thirty months old (believed to be at less risk of Mad Cow Disease)" (Shin, 2009: 569). According to Act on the Prevention of Contagious Animal Diseases, the terms and conditions of the partial import agreement were implemented by the Ministry of Agriculture in the form of a ministry notification (in Korean, *gosi*) (Shin, 2009: 569). The Korean law also requires that before any ministry introduces and implements a notification, it must publish the features of the notification to the public and solicit their opinions.[17] The Ministry of Agriculture followed the procedure under the law, and the notification took effect in March 2006 (2006 Notification).[18] The U.S. beef imports resumed, but shortly afterwards, the Roh Moo-Hyun government prohibited the importation again when pieces of bones were found in the imported U.S. beef (Lee, 2006). The Ministry of Agriculture held that "the inclusion of bone chips in the imported beef was a violation of the 2006 Notification" (Shin, 2009: 569). While U.S. exporters requested "reasonable bone chip tolerance" for future shipments, the Roh Moo-Hyun

[17] Korean Administrative Procedure Act, *supra* note 2, arts. 41–42.
[18] Ministry of Agriculture Notification, Health Conditions for Importing U.S. Beef, No. 2006-15 (Mar. 6, 2006).

government did not allow their requests (Shin, 2009: 569). The Korean Trade Minister stated that "the beef issue should not be viewed as [a] market access issue, but a national health issue" (Lee & Lee, 2005: 62). When bone chips were detected again in a shipment to Korea, the Roh Moo-Hyun government ordered a total ban on the U.S. beef imports in October 2007 in response to climbing public concerns about the repeated violations of the 2006 Notification by the U.S. beef exporters (Shin, 2007).

In May 2007, the World Organization for Animal Health (OIE) identified the U.S. as a "controlled risk" country for BSE (United States Department of Agriculture, 2007). Several U.S. government officials used this international validation to urge the Korean government to reopen export markets to the full spectrum of the U.S. beef products. In particular, the United States demanded that "Korea should expand the age limit of the cattle, allow boned meat, and relax the inspection standard so that minute issues like small bone chips do not trigger a suspension of imported U.S. beef" (Shin, 2009: 570).

The Beginning of the 2008 Korean Candlelight Vigil

As soon as conservative Lee Myung-Bak government began its term in 2008, its approach toward the U.S. beef import issue was rapidly changed. Influential U.S. lawmakers intensified the pressure on the Lee government and warned that they would not support the Korea-United States Free Trade Agreement (KORUS FTA) in Congress unless the Lee government resolved the beef import issue. One day before President Lee Myung-Bak was scheduled to meet President George W. Bush in April 2008, the Ministry of Food, Agriculture, Forestry, and Fisheries of Korea (2008) announced that the Korean government had agreed with the U.S. government to lift the import ban on U.S. beef.[19] As the implementation of the new U.S. beef

---

19 In February 2008, the Lee Myung-Bak government changed the name of the Ministry from the Ministry of Agriculture to the Ministry of Food, Agriculture, Forestry, and Fisheries.

import agreement required an amendment to the 2006 Notification, the Ministry published the highlights of the new agreement and sought public opinion based on Korean Administrative Procedure Act (Shin, 2009: 570).

When the contents of the new agreement were published for the public, they caused a huge dissent within Korean society. The Korean public requested to identify the basis for this significantly sudden shift in policy and asked whether the Lee government had carefully considered public health when it agreed to lift the import ban on U.S. beef and to relax the standards for inspection.

Furthermore, the Korean public's concerns were intensified due to an episode by an investigative TV program, *PD Notebook*, of the *Munhwa Broadcasting Corporation (MBC)*.[20] On April 29, 2008, in the episode about Mad Cow Disease associated with U.S. beef, *PD Notebook* reported that Koreans would be more genetically vulnerable to BSE than other ethnic groups.[21] Additionally, *PD Notebook* argued that the Lee Myung-Bak

---

20 The *Munhwa Broadcasting Corporation (MBC)* is one of four major national South Korean television and radio networks. *Munhwa* means "culture." The network is owned by the Foundation of Broadcast Culture, which has 70 percents of the company's stocks, while the Jung-Su Scholarship Association owns 30 percents. The *MBC* receives no government subsidies, and its income is earned entirely from commercial advertising. Currently, the *MBC* operates 19 local stations and 10 subsidiaries, with approximately 4,000 employees.

21 In March 2009, Chung Woon-Chun, who was the former Minister of the Ministry of Food, Agriculture, Forestry, and Fisheries, and Min Dong-Seok, who was a chief of beef deal negotiator, prosecuted five producers of *PD Notebook* for libel. They claimed that *PD Notebook* tainted their reputation by distorting and exaggerating the facts associated with Mad Cow Disease. However, in January 2010, an appellate court upheld a ruling clearing the five producers of *PD Notebook* of defamation charges. The court acknowledged that some interviews and comments of the host in the episode were either distorted or exaggerated to highlight the risk of Mad Cow Disease, but they fell short of punishing the producers because the intent was not malicious. The court said that the producers were modified some facts within legally tolerable degrees. "The media's role is watching and criticizing the government. These functions should be guaranteed more strongly when the media deals with an issue that is destined to affect a great number of people," said Judge Lee Sang-hoon. The judge said that this ruling was based on the presumption that a defamation case involving public figures should be judged by different criteria,

government's attempt to renegotiate the beef import with the U.S. without citizens' approval meant a violation of the right to health. This episode gave rise to a huge emotional response in the Korean people. The audiences linked the *PD Notebook* episode on their blogs and discussed it in online forums. In response, the Lee government explained that "the U.S. beef to be imported was the same safe beef that Americans consumed daily and that Korea had to accept the OIE international standard unless objective scientific grounds justified deviation from the OIE guidelines" (Shin, 2009: 570). Additionally, the Lee government continuously stressed that the new agreement would be a great opportunity in strengthening the Korean economy. However, it failed to ease the public's concerns.

Korean citizens started to hold candlelight vigils against the U.S. beef imports and demanded renegotiation of the agreement to reduce the scope of imported U.S. beef and to restore Korea's full right to inspection. The first vigil was started on May 2, 2008, by an online community named People's Movement to Impeach President Lee Myung-Bak and a group of high school girls who felt fearful that BSE infected beef would be served on their tables. These first candlelight vigil soon snowballed into a nationwide phenomenon (Lee, Kim, & Wainwright, 2010). A candlelight vigil was held everyday for first two months, and as of June 10, 2008, a weekend rally was continued in many different locations across the nation. During this period, a total of approximately one million Korean citizens (about 2 percent of all Koreans) participated in the candlelight protest (Amnesty International, 2008: 4).[22]

During the whole process of the 2008 Korean Candlelight Vigil, most collective actions were generated from everyday citizens' participation. The participants consisted of teenagers, college students, office workers, clergy, housewives and their children, unionists, members of several non-political online communities, reservist soldiers, and activist groups (Lee, Kim, &

interpreting freedom of expression more broadly.

[22] There were countless citizens who did not participated in the street protest but did engage in the "online protest" during the entire process of the 2008 Korean Candlelight Vigil.

Wainwright, 2010). This composition of the participants of the 2008 Korean Candlelight Vigil differed from many previous movements, such as Minjung Movement in the 1970s and 1980s and June Democracy Movement in 1987, whose main participants had been college students, laborers, and clergy (S. Kim, 2000). In particular, the majority of the participants in the 2008 Korean Candlelight Vigil were young liberal-progressives in their twenties and thirties, namely the post-386 liberal-progressives. One survey of the participants of the 2008 Korean Candlelight Vigil shows that 63.8% of the participants identified themselves as "liberal-progressive," while 7.3% and 28.9% of the participants identified themselves as "conservative" and "moderate," respectively. More than two-thirds (66.9%) was between the twenties and thirties (K. Cho, 2009).

In the early stage of the 2008 Korean Candlelight Vigil, the participants peacefully held the candlelight vigil to show their opposition to the Lee Myung-Bak government's decision on the U.S. beef imports, and the government also allowed the participants to hold the rally. However, as the government maintained its original plan for the resumption of the U.S. beef imports despite the objection from the public, the Korean citizens' collective actions gradually extended to a huge movement (An, 2010: 154). The participants opposed almost every government policy—such as the liberalization of public education, the Grand Canal project, and the privatization of the public sectors (i.e., water, health care, public enterprises, and public broadcasting)—and voiced their dissatisfaction with the general leadership of newly elected President Lee Myung-Bak (Kim et al., 2010).

At this stage, the Lee Myung-Bak government started considering whether the candlelight protest would potentially undermine public order, so the government labeled the rally as an illegal and violent demonstration. Based on the Assembly and Demonstration Act, the police's permission for the candlelight vigil was no longer granted anymore (UN Human Rights Council, 2011: 15). Every candlelight vigil was presumably illegal without the permission, and consequently, the Korean government could *legally* suppress the candlelight vigil.[23] On May 13, 2008, the Chief of the Korean National Police Agency, Uh Chung-Soo, said in a press conference that he was willing to use every method of suppression against the protesters. After this press conference, on May 24, 2008, thirty-six citizens were arrested by the police while they were marching through downtown Seoul. This was the first time the Korean police suppressed the candlelight protest, which had been peacefully going on for twenty-two days, since it began on May 2. In the course of cracking down on the candlelight protest, the combat police officers played a main role. The combat police officers followed orders to attack unarmed citizens and commit violent and cruel actions. The protesters were hit in the face by water cannons fired by the combat police officers from less than 10 meters away and consequently had their eardrums split. They were severely injured due to the subsequent attacks with shields and batons (Amnesty International, 2008: 10). The combat police officers also sprayed fire extinguishers toward the protesters' faces to impair the visibility of protesters during the suppression of the candlelight protest (Amnesty International, 2008: 11). The Lee Myung-Bak government justified this violent restriction as necessary to protect national security and national economic development. From May 24 to August 9, the Korean police made a total of 1,242 arrests, and approximately 2,000 citizens were injured (Amnesty International, 2008: 4).

Why did millions of Korean citizens voluntarily join such collective efforts at risk of arrest? How could they sustain their participation and lead the movement to achieve critical levels of support from the Korean public in the long enduring protest? The ostensible initial cause of the 2008 Korean Candlelight Vigil was the resumption of the U.S. beef imports. However, at

---

23 Although the Korean law guarantees the right to freedom of peaceful assembly based on article 21 of the Constitution, the government can prohibit peaceful assemblies that *are considered likely* to disturb public order (UN Human Rights Council, 2011). The Assembly and Demonstration Act provides that any person who desires to hold an outdoor assembly or a demonstration must submit a report to the chief of the competent police station with details regarding the planned event (article 6), who has the authority to ban an assembly or demonstration if it is deemed to pose a direct threat to public peace and order (article 8). Particularly, article 10 of the Assembly and Demonstration Act prohibits outdoor rallies after sunset without permission, except in cases where permission is obtained from the competent authorities.

its core root, the emergence and maintenance of the 2008 Korean Candlelight Vigil must be explained within the context of the long-term struggles of Korean citizens, particularly the liberal-progressives, for defining their position in Korean society.

In this chapter, I attempted to describe such struggles, by focusing on the process of developing the relationships among successive Korean governments, civil society, and media system. This process has particularly influenced the flow of information in the public sphere, and consequently, certain political actors have held a dominant position in Korean society through *symbolic power*—the capacity to shape or transform people's minds. The mainstream media have developed under the strong connection with the conservative forces and business imperatives, and these relationships have hindered diversity in the media discourse in Korea. Nonetheless, although a large portion of the news media has been still seen as part of the conservative bloc and supported the vested interest groups in Korea, the liberal-progressives have continuously attempted to transform the media system. The 2008 Korean Candlelight Vigil occurred within this context of an evolving set of ideas about the roles of citizens in the public sphere.

References

Amnesty International. (2008). *Policing the Candlelight Protests in South Korea*. London: Amnesty International Publications.

An, S. (2010). The rise of networked individualism and the possibility of new democracy: A case study of the 2008 Candlelight Protest in South Korea. *Journal of Cyber Society and Culture*, 1(1): 145–175.

Chae, H., & Kim, S. (2008). Conservatives and progressives in South Korea. *Washington Quarterly*, 31(4): 77–95.

Chang, W.-Y. (2005). Online civic participation, and political empowerment: Online media and public opinion formation in Korea. *Media, Culture & Society*, 27(6): 925–935.

Cho, D. (1997). *The Korean Chaebol*. Seoul: Maeilkyungje Shinmun-Sa.

Cho, G. M. (2005). *Study on Marriage Chains among Korean Media Owners*. Master of Arts Thesis, Korea University, Seoul.

Cho, K. (1997). Tension between the national security law and constitutionalism in outh Korea: Security for what? *Boston University International Law Journal*, 15: 125–174.

_____ (2009). The ideological orientation of 2008 candlelight vigil participants: Anti-American, pro-North Korean left or anti-neoliberalism? *The Korean Political Science Review*, 43(3): 125–148.

Choi, J. J. (2005). *Democracy after democratization: The Korean experience*. Seoul: Humanitas.

Doucette, J. (2012). The Korean Thermidor: On political space and conservative reactions. *Transactions of the Institute of British Geographers*. doi: 10.1111/j.1475-5661.2012. 00528.x

Fairclough, G. (2004, April 14). Generation why?: The 386ers of Korea question old rules, *The Wall Street Journal*. Retrieved from https://www.wsj.com/articles/SB10818944569 5281806

GI Korea. (2008). GI Flashbacks: The 2002 Armored vehicle accident, *ROK Drop*. Retrieved from http://www.rokdrop.net/2008/06/gi-flashback-2002-armored-vehicle-accident/

Gillmor, D. (2006). *We the Media: Grassroots Journalism by the People, for the People*. Sebastopol, CA: O'Reilly Media.

Gluck, C. (2003, March 12). South Korea's web guerrillas, *BBC News*. Retrieved from http://news.bbc.co.uk/2/hi/asia-pacific/2843651.stm

Han, S.-K. (2008). Breadth and depth of unity among Chaebol families in Korea. *Korean Journal of Sociology*, 42(4): 1–25.

Im, S.-K., & Kim, Y.-B. (2004, March 4). Roh openly supports the Uri Party, *The Hankyoreh*. Retrieved from http://news.naver.com/main/read.nhn?oid=028&aid=0000 048424

Im, S.-K., & Yi, H.-J. (2004, May 14). 84% approve the Constitutional Court's dismissal, *The Hankyoreh*. Retrieved from http://www.hani.co.kr/section-003500000/2004/05/ 003500000200405142318950.html

Jang, S. (2006). The Internet age: Journalist's information power is changing. In H.

Walravens (ed.). *Newspapers of the World Online: U.S. and International Perspectives* (pp. 179–190). München: K.G.Saur.

Jo, S., & Kim, Y. (2004). Media or personal relations?: Exploring media relations dimensions in South Korea. *Journalism & Mass Communication Quarterly*, 81(2): 292–306.

Kang, J. (2009). Coming to terms with "unreasonable" global power: The 2002 South Korean Candlelight Vigils. *Communication and Critical/Cultural Studies*, 6(2): 171–192.

Kang, J. M. (2002). The birth of the conservative newspapers: The 1980s. *People and Ideology*, 55: 118–135.

Kim, C., Lee, H., Kim, S., & Lee, C. (2010). Changing social attitudes of teenager participants of 2008 Candlelight Vigil: What happened to them after an year? *Economy and Society*, 85: 265–290.

Kim, D., & Johnson, T. J. (2006). A victory of the Internet over mass media?: Examining the effects of online media on political attitudes in South Korea. *Asian Journal of Communication*, 16(1): 1–18.

Kim, E.-G., & Hamilton, J. W. (2006). Capitulation to capital? OhmyNews as alternative media. *Media, Culture & Society*, 28(4): 541–560.

Kim, H., Choi, J. Y., & Cho, J. (2008). Changing cleavage structure in new democracies: An empirical analysis of political cleavages in Korea. *Electoral Studies*, 27(1): 136–150.

Kim, J. U. (2000). The generation of the Korean media colglomerates. *Contemporary Critics*, 10: 106–126.

Kim, S.-S. (2002). Rethinking newspaper ownership, control and media power. *Journal of Korean Society for Journalism and Communication Studies*, 46(2): 122–149.

Kim, S. (2000). *The Politics of Democratization in Korea: The Role of Civil Society*. Pittsburgh, PA: The University of Pittsburgh Press.

Kim, Y.-H. (2001). The broadcasting audience movement in Korea. *Media, Culture & Society*, 23(1): 91–107.

Kirk, D. (2001a, May 7). South Korea's conservative press takes heat from the liberals, *The New York Times*. Retrieved from https://www.nytimes.com/2001/05/07/world/south-korea-s-conservative-press-takes-heat-from-the-liberals.html

_____ (2001b, August 18). South Korean news executives are arrested on tax charges, *The New York Times*. Retrieved from https://www.nytimes.com/2001/08/18/world/south-korean-news-executives-are-arrested-on-tax-charges.html

_____ (2008). South Korea's National Security Law: A tool of oppression in an insecure world. *Wisconsin International Law Journal*, 24(2): 627–659.

Lee, J. (2009). *Net Power in Action: Internet Activism in the Contentious Politics of South Korea*. Doctoral dissertation, Rutgers, The State University of New Jersey, New Brunswick.

Lee, J., & Lee, H. (2005). *Feasibility and Economic Effects of a Korea-U.S. FTA*. Seoul: Korea Institute for International Economic Policy.

Lee, K. (2003). Pressures for media reform in Korea: There are loud calls for changes in the way the press and government interact. *Nieman Reports*, 57(4): 93–95.

Lee, N. (2007). *The making of minjung: Democracy and the politics of representation in South*

Korea. Ithaca, NY: Cornell University Press.

Lee, S. (2006, November 16). The U.S. beef imports are detained in quarantine, *OhmyNews*. Retrieved from http://media.daum.net/society/affair/view.html?cateid=1010&newsid =20061116220309800&p=ohmynews

Lee, S., Kim, S., & Wainwright, J. (2010). Mad cow militancy: Neoliberal hegemony and social resistance in South Korea. *Political Geography*, 29: 359–369.

Lee, Y. (2005). Law, politics, and impeachment: The impeachment of Roh Moo-hyun from a comparative constitutional perspective. *American Journal of Comparative Law*, 53: 403–432.

Oh, S. (2008). The increase of influence and credibility of the Internet. *Newspapers & Broadcasting*, 451: 146–149.

Oh, Y.-H. (2004). *The Speciality of Korea: OhmyNews*. Seoul: Humanist.

Paik, N. C. (2007). Democracy and peace in Korea twenty years after June 1987: Where are we now, and where do we go from here? *The Asia-Pacific Journal: Japan Focus*, 3. Retrieved from http://www.japanfocus.org/-Nak_chung-Paik/2440

Park, M. J., Kim, C. N., & Sohn, B. W. (2000). Modernization, globalization, and the powerful state: The Korean media. In J. Curran & M. J. Park (eds.). *De-Westernizing media studies* (pp. 111–123). New York, NY: Routledge.

Rhee, I.-Y. (2003). The Korean election shows a shift in media power: Young voters create a 'cyber Acropolis' and help to elect the president. *Nieman Reports*, 57(1): 95–96.

Sa, E. S. (2009a). Development of press freedom in South Korea since Japanese colonial rule. *Asian Culture and History*, 1(2): 3–17.

____ (2009b). Factors influencing freedom of the press in South Korea: A survey of print Journalists' opinions. *Asian Social Science*, 5(3): 3–24.

Shim, D. (2002). South Korean media industry in the 1990s and the economic crisis. *Prometheus*, 20(4): 337–350.

Shin, E. H. (2005). Presidential elections, internet politics, and citizens' organizations in South Korea. *Development and Society*, 34(1): 25–47.

Shin, H. (2007, August 2). The U.S. beef imports is prohibited again, *Yonhap News*. Retrieved from http://media.daum.net/economic/industry/view.html?cateid=1038& newsid=20070802135412029&p=yonhap

Shin, H.-T. (2009). The domestic decisionmaking process and its implications for international commitments: American beef in Korea. *The Yale Journal of International Law*, 34: 567–574.

Shirky, C. (2008). *Here Comes Everybody: The Power of Organizing without Organizations*. New York, NY: Penguin Books.

Steinberg, D. I., & Shin, M. (2006). Tensions in South Korean political parties in transition: From entourage to ideology? *Asian Survey*, 46(4): 517–537.

UN Human Rights Council. (2011). Report of the Special Rapporteur on the promotion and protection of the right to freedom of opinion and expression, Frank La Rue: addendum: mission to the Republic of Korea: United Nations Human Rights Council.

Yang, S.-M. (2005). Democratization and media reform: The case of South Korea. In C. Schafferer (ed.). *Understanding Eodern East Asian Politics* (pp. 19–35). New York, NY: Nova Science Publishers.

Yoon, D.-K. (2010). *Law and Democracy in South Korea: Democratic Development Since 1987.* Seoul: The Institute for Far Eastern Studies, Kyungnam University.

Youm, K.-H. (1996). *Press law in South Korea.* Iowa City: Iowa State University Press.

A Constitutive Moment in the Korean Journalistic Culture

2

WOOYEOL SHIN

The Korea Center for Investigative Journalism

Over the last decade, the journalistic culture in South Korea has been entering an unsettled period (Swidler, 1986). In this constitutive moment of the journalistic culture, the naturalness of the dominant logic of journalism has been challenged. A large segment of Korean society has questioned the established role of Korean journalism and sought to transform it. In this process, the meaning of journalism has been contested in Korean society. In this chapter, I discuss the public reaction to the dominant culture of journalism, especially the instrumental view of journalism. The instrumental view inside and outside journalism undermines the stability of the journalistic community as well as the trust between journalists and the public. This chapter also introduces an emerging model of journalism—nonprofit, citizen funded journalism. The challenge of Korean news nonprofits to the dominant logic of journalism is a process of setting an alternative evaluation criterion for the performance of Korean journalists.

To discuss these, I analyzed 10 books published by main actors of the Press Freedom Movement in the 2010s, including former journalists who were forced to resign by mainstream news media during the 2010s and bloggers. In addition, I collected a specific set of tweets containing the term 기레기 (*giraegi*), by monitoring Twitter's public streaming API between

December 2014 and March 2015. By interrogating these tweets, I tried to show how Koreans Twitter users speak about journalism in this unsettled period.

"THE SECOND DARK AGE" OF KOREAN JOURNALISM

Korean journalism has become one of the most contentious issues in Korean society since the inauguration of the conservative President Lee Myung-bak in 2008. A wide range of citizens have explicitly revealed their antipathy to mainstream journalists, especially criticizing the democratic deficits in the media system. In particular, most of this criticism has been targeted at the performance of three national broadcasters—two public broadcasters, the *Korean Broadcasting System* (*KBS*) and the *Munhwa Broadcasting Corporation* (*MBC*), and the 24-hour news channel *Yonhap Television Network* (*YTN*).

Between the late 1990s and mid 2000s, before the beginning of the Lee Myung-bak presidency, the news staff of these national broadcasters enjoyed the maximum level of journalistic freedom both from the state and from the executives of their corporations in Korean journalism history. During the two successive administrations of democratic-progressive Presidents Kim Dae-jung (1998–2003) and Roh Moo-hyun (2004–2008), the views of the presidents on journalism were significantly different from those of the former presidents, especially the military dictators. In particular, President Roh Moo-hyun attempted to remove many conventional privileges that the government had enjoyed over the news media. For example, Roh Moo-hyun provided government officials with a not-to-do list to remove the conventional practices between the officials and journalists. Roh advised the public affairs officials not to offer any favor to beat reporters, as well as their editors, so that favorable news stories about the government would be produced. In addition, the Roh government decided to close the offices for the press clubs, called *gijasil*, in government branch organizations, including the Blue House. As explained in Chapter II, these press club offices had been considered integral to the relations between the government and the news media. Roh believed that these top-down attempts to reform the journalistic culture could dismantle the existing collusion between government officials and beat reporters.

In this period, the public broadcasting system was largely insulated from government control and operated by broadcasting professionals. During the Roh Moo-hyun administration, for example, government officials were told not to underhandedly contact the public broadcasting corporations to complain about the stories of the government (Lee, 2003). According to the then *KBS* president Yeonju Jeong (2011), President Roh also promised Jeong that he would never call Jeong during his presidency because he wanted the *KBS* to be a fair and independent institution (Jeong, 2011: 361–362). Senior broadcasting reporter Seo also emphasized that during the Roh Moo-hyun's term "it was possible that every news corporation could criticize and even insult the current President without fear of future reprisal for the first time in Korean history" (personal communication, October 5, 2014).

In this process of differentiation from the state, the growth of professional norms and practices was observed in the public broadcasting corporations. In 2005, for instance, an investigative reporting unit was established in the *KBS*. The founder of this unit was then-*KBS* reporter Youngjin Kim. Youngjin Kim and his unit members researched, upheld, and practiced the principles and methods of investigative reporting developed in other news organizations, such as Investigative Reporters and Editors, Inc. (IRE), and consequently received dozens of prestigious national and international journalism awards during the Roh Moo-hyun presidency. Based on this increased degree of professionalism, several broadcasting journalists I interviewed identified the 2000s as "the golden age of Korean broadcasting journalism."

On the contrary, the degree of political parallelism of newspaper companies has become higher since the two successive democratic-progressive presidencies. The Kim Dae-jung and Roh Moo-hyun governments attempted to reform the news media industry and in this process publicly criticized the performance of mainstream conservative newspapers, particularly the *Chosun*, the *Joongang*, and the *Dong-A* (Jie & Lee, 2012: 266–267).

For many Koreans, especially for the conservatives, these top-down efforts by the two governments were considered a severe violation of press freedom. Indeed, the term "press freedom" and the way to achieve press freedom have been instrumentalized by different political parties.

The golden age ended with the inauguration of President Lee Myung-bak in 2008. As discussed in the previous chapter, in Korean society, the level of freedom of individual journalists of the public broadcasting corporations from the interference of the state is largely determined by the president's perspective on journalism. This is because the government has the policy measures to influence the personnel management of the national broadcasters (Choi & Jie, 2014: 22). The Lee government openly and secretly attempted to control the public broadcasting system. First, See-joong Choi, who was a close friend of President Lee's older brother and also President Lee's political mentor, was appointed as the president of the Korean Communications Commission (KCC). As a media regulation government agency, the KCC has a legal authority not only to influence the appointments of the presidents of the *KBS* and the *MBC*, but also to manage and license the electromagnetic spectrum for commercial media companies and public media companies. The appointment of See-joong Choi, therefore, was considered "a tactical appointment" by the Lee government to control the broadcasting industry (Jeong, 2011: 92–94; Roh, 2012: 86–89). Along with the appointment of Choi as the KCC president, in 2008, the chief executives and presidents of several media corporations—including the *KBS*, the *MBC*, the *YTN*, the *Korean Broadcasting Advertising Corporation* (KOBACO), the *Arirang TV*, and the *Sky Life*—were also replaced by supporters of President Lee Myung-bak (Amnesty International, 2009).[1]

1 There is some evidence that the Lee Myung-bak government monitored the appointment processes of the chief executives and presidents of the media corporations, especially the *KBS* and the *YTN*. The Bureau of Civil Service Discipline and Investigation (BCSDI), an agency monitoring public officials for possible corruption, carried out missions to monitor the inside affairs of the national broadcasters, especially the performances of the presidents of the national broadcasters (Choe, 2012). First, according to the BCSDI reports disclosed by the *KBS* union members, the *KBS* was under the BCSDI's

In particular, three former aides of President Lee were elected as the presidents of three leading broadcasting corporations, the *KBS*, the *MBC*, and the *YTN*. *KBS* president Ingyu Kim and *YTN* president Bon-hong Ku had participated in the Lee Myung-bak's presidential campaign as the communications director and the special advisor on broadcasting, respectively. *MBC* president Jaecheol Kim was also known as a close acquaintance of President Lee Myung-bak since he had served as a *MBC* political reporter. These three presidents had experienced the military authoritarian rule as journalists and survived the Purification Campaign of the Chun military regime. *KBS* president Ingyu Kim, for example, began his journalistic career at the *KBS* in 1973. Kim has been criticized by media critics because he produced several news reports idealizing the authoritarian rule of the Chun regime. He served in many top positions at the *KBS*, such as a US correspondent and news director, and became a news executive in 2003. In 2007, Kim resigned from the executive position of the *KBS* to participate in the presidential campaign of Lee Myung-bak.

This situation particularly affected those journalists who had begun their

surveillance. The BCSDI was monitoring the union's activities, evaluating the *KBS* president's performance, and predicting a possible result of the president's personnel management. In particular, the BCSDI recommended that the *KBS* president Kim Ingyu had to be "more careful and modest in his behavior and speech" in order to "advance the unity and cohesion of the *KBS* employees and ultimately promote the reform of the *KBS*" (Newstapa, 2012). Secondly, the BCSDI also engaged in the appointment process of the *YTN* president in 2009. The BCSDI, for example, evaluated the acting president Bae Seok-kyu as "loyal to the current government" and praised his enterprising spirit as follows: "Bae Seok-kyu is dedicated himself to reform the *YTN* . . . as shown in recent cases of personnel management . . . such as the abolition of the direct election of editor-in-chief . . . and the replacements of left-leaning editor-in-chief, anchormen, and pro-union executives" (Newstapa, 2012). Based on this evaluation, the BCSDI recommended that "the government used its influence over the [*YTN*]'s major shareholders to help make [Bae Seok-kyu] president" (Choe, 2012). Although it is unclear whether the government had actually forced the *YTN* shareholders—the government enterprises—to elect Bae Seok-kyu as the president, Bae Seok-kyu was elected and was serving as the *YTN* president between 2009 and 2015. This BCSDI scandal was described by *The New York Times* as "Echoes of Watergate" on April 9, 2012 (see Choe, 2012).

journalistic careers after the collapse of the military regime and enjoyed the process of the progressive development of journalistic freedom. For these journalists, the comebacks of these older journalists-turned-politicians, whom they called "living fossils," were seen as a regression to the old, authoritarian measures of the state to control the news media industry. As former *KBS* investigative reporter Omin Gwon told me, "It seemed virtually impossible that these President's men, what we call 'parachute appointees,' could be independent from the Lee government. They would be seduced by President Lee, intimidated by him, and finally compromised by their own political interests." He continued to stress the potential consequences of the appointments of the "President's men":

> The history of the military control over the news media caused permanent trauma to Korean journalism. This is a kind of *institutional post-traumatic stress disorder*, I think. We continuously suffer from the possibility of government interference in editorial independence. We learn from our history what will happen if journalists collectively experience the government's control. I really don't want to be part of that tragedy. I don't want to experience the situation in which I can't write a story that I like to write. In particular, I really don't want to be like those pseudo-journalists. (personal communication, November 28, 2014)

This fear provoked severe objections from the news staff of the public broadcasters. In July 2008, the union members of the *YTN* went on strike to protest the elected president Bon-hong Ku and call for guarantees of editorial independence. *YTN*'s struggle continued until April 2009. During this struggle, six journalists were dismissed by the *YTN* in October 2008. Four of them, including *YTN* union chairman Jong-myun Roh, were arrested for "interfering with business" in March 2009. Many peer journalists both from the *YTN* and other news companies expressed their objection to the dismissal decisions made by the *YTN*'s executives. In particular, broadcasting reporters and anchors conducted the so-called "Black Struggle" (Roh, 2012: 62–66). They agreed to all wear a black suit while recording a news program. A black suit symbolized the days of the military dictatorship when color television broadcasting had not been introduced yet.[2] In other words, by wearing a black suit, these journalists intended to express their objection to the conventional views of the Lee government and its aides on the news media (Roh, 2012: 65).

The reporters' dismissal and arrest drew international attention to the *YTN* strike (e.g., Amnesty International, 2009; International Federation of Journalists, 2009). Between 2008 and 2009, Amnesty International researchers met with the *YTN* union members to review their claims of unwarranted government interference in editorial independence. Frank La Rue, the United Nations Special Rapporteur on the promotion and protection of the right to freedom of opinion and expression, also undertook an official mission to the Republic of Korea in May 2010 and reported as follows:

> [The] Special Rapporteur expresses his concern that . . . there have been increased restrictions on individuals' right to freedom of opinion and expression, primarily due to an increasing number of prosecutions, based on laws that are often not in conformity with international standards, of individuals who express views which are not in agreement with the position of the Government. . . . The Special Rapporteur stresses the importance of ensuring that the independence of heads and management of broadcasting corporations be guaranteed through an effective appointment process (La Rue, 2011: 1–2, 18).

This national and international attention given to the Lee government and Korean journalism, however, did not guarantee the independence of the news staff of the public broadcasting corporations from their executives and also from the government. Borrowing from Merrill's (1993) concepts, this

---

2 In South Korea, the Chun Doo-hwan military regime introduced color television on December 1, 1980, right after the mass dismissal of around 930 journalists under the Purification Campaign.

situation in Korean journalism could be seen as a lack of "journalistic freedom." Merrill (1993) argued that it would be important to distinguish journalistic freedom from press freedom. According to him, "press freedom concerns a relationship between the press and the government," while "journalistic freedom concerns a relationship between the journalists working for a news medium and the executives and editors of that news medium" (pp. 34–35). Korean journalism scholar Jae-kyung Lee (1997) also suggested that a distinction needs to be made between "publisher's freedom" and "reporters' freedom" (p. 137). In this sense, the veteran broadcasting producer Seungho Choi evaluated the level of journalistic freedom in the late 2000s and the 2010s as "almost comparable with that under the military regimes" (Choi & Jie, 2014: 83). "This period will be called the second dark age in Korean journalism history," Choi added (Choi & Jie, 2014: 82).[3]

In particular, since 2010 when Jaecheol Kim was appointed as the *MBC* president, the *MBC* staff was faced with the most blatant interference by management with regard to the news selection and production process. The *MBC* union was on strike between April and June 2010 to protest the appointment of Jaecheol Kim as the *MBC* president. However, the strike ended with the dismissal of the *MBC* union chairman Geun-haeng Lee and pay cuts and/or the temporary suspension of the work of several union executives. After the end of the strike, the executives of the *MBC* abolished the Bureau of Current Affairs and Education that had produced investigative news magazine programs. As a result, the current affairs show *News Who* was cancelled. Several producers and reporters who had produced these news magazine programs were transferred to the sports department, the sales department, the traffic department, or the *MBC*'s regional stations. In the *MBC*'s prime time daily news program *MBC News Desk*, several current affairs stories, including the scandal of the Gyeonggi Province Governor

---

3 Freedom House (2011), a US-based international NGO, also downgraded South Korea's media freedom rating from "free" in 2007 to "partly free" in 2011. According to Freedom House (2011), since the inauguration of President Lee Myung-Bak, "South Korea has experienced a noticeable decline in the freedom of expression for both journalists and the general public."

Moon-soo Kim and the scandal of President Lee's private residence, were killed, censored, or modified by the pro-government executives (Park, 2014: 99). At this point, the *MBC* started to be called *"M-Bing-Sin,"* literally meaning stupid *MBC* (Park, 2014: 99). In November 2011, at an anti U.S.-Korea Free Trade Agreement (FTA) protest site, *MBC* reporters were denied access to the protesters and were finally expelled by the protesters from the protest site. The protesters believed that the *MBC* would twist the issue under government pressure or not be able to publish the issue anyhow (Jo, 2011).

After this incident, *MBC* reporters held votes of confidence in the general meeting of the association of reporters to remove the news editor-in-chief and news director from the newsroom. When the association of *MBC* reporters announced the result that a majority of *MBC* reporters issued a vote of no confidence, the executives of the *MBC* immediately penalized the head of the association of reporters. In response to this company's decision, on January 25, 2012, *MBC* reporters started to boycott news production. This was the beginning of a series of strikes by the news staff of several news companies.

A total of approximately 1,300 media workers of the *MBC* were on strike for 170 days between January 30 and July 17, 2012. The media workers of the *KBS*, the *YTN*, the *Yonhap News Agency*, and the *Kookmin Ilbo* subsequently went on strike. The main purposes of these strikes were to force the president of each company to resign from office and to enhance the news staff's editorial independence. The news staff at the public broadcasting networks also requested a revision of the procedures to appoint their presidents to increase the autonomy of the networks. The *KBS* union members also required the company to restore the investigative reporting unit that had been abolished by the pro-government executives, while the *YTN* strikers called on the *YTN* executives to reinstate the six dismissed reporters.

During the strikes, the union members also actively used digital media, such as social networking sites and podcasting/vodcasting, not only to tell stories about the strikes but also to produce news stories about current affairs. In particular, each of the union members of the *KBS*, the *MBC*, and the *YTN* created their own podcasts to criticize their news corporations. These podcasts produced by the strikers, such as *Angry YTN*, *Reset KBS News 9*, *Real MBC News Desk* (*jedaero nyuseu deseukeu*), and *Power-Up PD Notebook* (*pawoeop pidi sucheop*), had an immense popularity among Koreans, especially younger democratic-progressives.[4] Koreans also supported the strikers through petition drives, fundraising concerts, and candlelight vigils, which is one of the most popular forms of collective actions in South Korea (Choi, 2012).

Nonetheless, the strikes failed to make any significant change in the news corporations and especially in the corporations' relations with the government. While the reporters continued to boycott news production, some news corporations hired temporary reporters to fill the news hole rather than accepted the requirements of the strikers. The pro-government presidents kept their positions, and several news staff members following the corporations' order were promoted to higher positions. Meanwhile, 455 journalists were penalized not only for participating in the strikes and interfering with business, but also for producing critical reports about their own news organizations and publishing them online. During Lee Myung-Bak's presidency between 2008 and 2013, a total of 21 journalists were fired from the *MBC*, the *YTN*, the *Kookmin Ilbo*, and the *Busan Ilbo* (National Union of Media Workers, 2013a). This mass dismissal of journalists by the news media was

---

4 This popularity of the strikers' vodcasts was in part attributed to the so-called "podcast phenomenon." As explained in the previous chapter, the civil society has continuously attempted to create and appropriate an alternative means of communication while most mainstream news media have maintained a collusive relationship with the state. In 2011, since a political satire podcast, The *Naneun Ggomsuda*—or the *I'm a Petty-Minded Creep* —gained huge popularity among Koreans, especially younger democratic-progressives, the podcast phenomenon began in early 2011. The *Naneun Ggomsuda* was the most downloaded podcast on *iTunes* globally in 2011 and 2012 (Jung, 2012), and each episode of this podcast was downloaded more than two million times (Choe, 2011). Since then, the podcasting medium has been employed as a form of alternative news. In particular, the current or former journalists who were fired or demoted from mainstream news corporations have actively appropriated the podcasting medium as needed to suit their particular objectives and values.

the first case since the end of the military dictatorship in 1987 (Roh, 2012: 56–62).

During the 2012 general election and the 2012 presidential election, most journalists who engaged in the strikes supported the democratic-progressive party and its Presidential candidate Moon Jae-in. They expected that Moon Jae-in would appoint more neutral, in their view, presidents of the public broadcasters. Since the state had continued to have policy measures to govern the media system, these journalists may have had no choice but to rely on political power to make a significant change in the structure of the media system. However, in opposition to their expectations, in both elections, the conservative Saenuri party won. In the 2012 general election, the conservative Saenuri Party became the ruling party in the National Assembly again by winning 152 out of the 300 Assembly seats, while the liberal-progressive New Politics Alliance for Democracy (*saejeongchi-minju-yeonhap*) won 127 seats. In addition, the conservative Presidential candidate Park Geun-hye, who is a daughter of the former dictator Park Jung-hee and was the former head of the conservative party, was elected as the 18th President of South Korea.

The failure of the strikes, as well as the victories of the conservative party in both elections, has led to intensifying the instrumentalization of journalism by the state. Under the consecutive conservative governments between 2008 and the present, the mainstream news media's, including public broadcasting corporations', support for the conservative political force has become more conspicuous (Rhee & Kim, 2012). During the Park Geun-hye's presidential campaign, the reform of the power structure between the government and the public broadcasting system and thereby the securing of the public broadcasting system's autonomy were Park's campaign promises. However, since her inauguration in 2013, the media policy of the Park Geun-hye government has not been significantly different from that of the Lee Myung-bak government. In particular, the president and the ruling party still have policy measures to influence the appointments of the presidents of public broadcasting corporations and therefore to impact their editorial stances (Jeongguk Lee, 2015).

AN UNSETTLED CULTURAL PERIOD OF KOREAN JOURNALISM

In this circumstance, the Korean journalistic culture has been entering an unsettled period, a period in which the dominant logic of Korean journalism is collapsing. These days, Korean journalists have been faced with an unprecedented challenge to their established roles as journalists.

This challenge to the journalistic system has been coming from ordinary citizens, especially from so-called "the members of the post-386 generation," equipped with digital technologies.[5] The post-386 generation is generally considered those Koreans who were born in the 1970s and the 1980s and entered the universities in the 1990s and the 2000s. The members of the post-386 generation have been regarded by older generations as an extremely egocentric and politically apathetic generation. However, through organizing and participating in a series of massive political and cultural events—such as the street cheering in the 2002 Korea-Japan World Cup soccer match, the 2002 Candlelight Vigil after the deaths of two middle school girls, the 2004 Candlelight Vigil against the impeachment of President Roh Moo-hyun, the 2008 Candlelight Vigil against the U.S. beef imports, the national funeral for the former President Roh Moo-hyun, and the 2014 Candlelight Vigil for the deaths of the victims of the Sewol ferry disaster—the members of the post-386 generation have constructed a collective generational consciousness and emerged as a crucial collective agent of political and cultural change in Korean society. They, in particular, have actively appropriated digital media to produce and share their opinions and to participate in political actions.

---

5 Coined in the 1990s, the 386 generation refers to those who were in their 30s, entered the universities in the 1980s, and were born in the 1960s. The 386 generation had played a crucial role as the force of student power in the Minjung Movement in the 1980s and the June Democracy Movement that terminated decades of two military regimes in 1987. Members of the 386 generation have been considered more skeptical of the United States compared with the older generations. This is largely because the U.S. had "backed the same military regimes they had fought against" (Fairclough, 2004). Growing into their 40s by the 2000s, they began to hold important positions in politics and business.

The desire of the post-386 generation for media reform has lasted long since they took the key role in political movements. In many political events, they have stood in opposition to mainstream news media, especially to the "Big Three Newspapers." These mainstream news media have been active agents in constructing meanings for the political movements, usually describing them as very different from how the participants of the movements understand their movements. For example, in the 2008 Candlelight Vigil, while the vigil participants identified the protest as a "peaceful," "democratic," and "nonviolent resistance," the Big Three Newspapers, namely the *Chosun*, the *JoongAng*, and the *Dong-A*, called it a "violent," "bad," and "illegal" protest (Shin, 2016b). Thus, media activism has often become one of the main purposes of the political movements organized by the democratic-progressives. The aforementioned strikes by the news staff during the Lee Myung-bak administration were also widely supported by the members of the post-386 generation.

This grassroots efforts gained momentum during the Sewol ferry tragedy in 2014. During the rescue process, the coverage by the Korean media outlets was egregious. Right after the accident on April 16, 2014, most mainstream news outlets, including the country's two largest broadcast television networks, reported breaking news based on the government's announcement, saying that all the passengers were rescued. However, this information was wrong. This caused not only confusion and pain to the public and the families of the ferry victims in particular, but also slowed down the rescue process (Nam, 2014). Further, during the rescue process, the media outlets continued to report incorrect and misleading information based on the government's announcements and press statements without double-checking. The rules on disaster coverage suggested by the Journalists Association of Korea were repeatedly and collectively ignored by most mainstream media outlets. Inappropriate questions, for instance, were often asked by journalists to just-rescued high-school students during interviews (Um, 2014).

These wrongdoings and moral failure of journalists triggered public anger over Korean journalism and its collusive relationship with the political forces. Many Koreans, even journalists themselves and the families of the victims in particular, believed that the wrong and improper coverage of the incident hampered the rescue process and thereby that the Korean journalistic community was responsible for the deaths of the passengers (Nam, 2014). This reporting behavior of Korean journalists was considered a signal for the collective incompetency of Korean journalists. A survey by the Asan Institute for Policy Studies (as cited in Friedhoff, 2014), conducted in the end of April 2014, indicated public confidence in the media had declined to a record low.

At this point, a particular type of metajournalistic discourse arose from the public: The discourse of *giraegi*. The word *giraegi* is a combination of *gija*, the Korean word for a journalist or reporter, and *tsuraegi*, the Korean word for garbage. The word *giraegi* thus literally means a journalist who produces garbage rather than reports news. In this sense, the discourse of *giraegi* can be seen as a particular set of symbolic practices defining, evaluating, and offending Korean journalists and their established culture. In and through the discourse of *giraegi*, a wide range of Koreans started to ridicule mainstream journalists and their news products. They also actively assessed the quality of news stories published by news companies and expressed their anger toward the conspicuous support for the political forces. They have also started to create their own criteria to identify *good* and *bad journalism* and *good* and *bad journalists*. In other words, constitutive choices (Starr, 2004), those social choices that create a new logic for Korean journalism, have started to be made.

THE DISCOURSE OF *GIRAEGI*

The term *giraegi* first emerged around 2010 in response to the malpractices of Korean journalists online (Kim, 2013). At that time, the term was used by a few internet users to identify those journalists who repeatedly produce click-bait headlines and attention-grabbing stories to increase web traffic.[6] However, since the disastrously poor, unethical performance of Korean journalists during the rescue process of the Sewol ferry tragedy between April and May 2014, the term *giraegi* has been widely used to name any journalist practicing bad journalism.

These days, *giraegi* is synonymous with a *bad* Korean journalist. Whenever people become upset or uncomfortable by reading or watching a news report, they just call the reporter producing that news report a *giraegi*. On Twitter, for example, by using the hashtag *#giraegi*, tweets like "Working hard, *#giraegi!*," "Ugh! As expected, *#giraegi* did it again," or "Stupid *#giraegi*," are easily detected. In particular, the following two satirical scripts, tweeted everyday by an anti-*giraegi* Twitter account called @giraegi_bot, well reflect the public perception of Korean journalists these days:

> Executive of a news company: How can I help you?
> Applicant: I want to be a reporter.
> Executive of a news company: Why should I hire you?
> Applicant: I can speak in Korean.
> Executive of a news company: You are hired!
> #giraegi

> Son: Mom?
> Mom: What?
> Son: I don't have a dream.

6   In many traditional news outlets, according to several journalists I interviewed, the positions in the online news department or the digital products department are considered "a place of exile." In many cases, once a journalist is assigned to the online news department, she/he immediately starts to think of moving to other first-line positions, such as political editors and reporters. Since the business performance of the online news department is evaluated by online advertising revenue, the staff members need to increase Web traffic if they will "successfully and quickly" move to other departments in which they want to work. Consequently, the staff members of the online news department competitively create click-bait headlines and attention-grabbing stories and even use "bots" to increase Web traffic. For more detailed information about this—what is called "abusing journalism" in Korea—visit the Korean blogger DoDo's blog (http://blog.newstapa.org/enki; accessed on March 7, 2015).

Mom: OK, then, I encourage you to be a reporter.
#giraegi

Then, what is specifically called a *giraegi*-like journalistic practice? According to my analysis of the tweets containing the term *giraegi*, four interrelated patterns are detected. First, when journalists seem to be more loyal to their sources rather than to citizens, Koreans call them *giraegi*s. In particular, Koreans criticize those journalists who do not serve as an independent monitor of political and economic power-holders. For example, the tweets like "Most news media are not able to investigate wrongdoing by the current government. These disqualified media self-certify the fact that they are *giraegi*" or "Hey *giraegi*! Your job is scrutinizing possible abuses of power by the National Assembly in terms of its authority to decide the national budget, not serving as public relations devices of the lawmakers!" were affective expressions aimed at emphasizing the journalists' watchdog role. In addition, many Korean Twitter users assess possible connotations of the words or sentences written by journalists and then address the problem of political or ideological bias. For example, the use of an adjective by journalists to describe the activity of President Park Geun-hye was ridiculed as follows: "Have anyone seen the *YTN*'s report about Park Geun-hye yet? This *giraegi* says, 'President Park has proven herself to be an *attractive* President at the summit conference.' This *giraegi* even highlights the term 'attractive'! So ridiculous!" Furthermore, when journalists seem to be used as a tool of powerful institutions, especially the government, many Koreans call them "government-kept-journalists" (*eoyong-gija*), "politicized journalists" (*jeongchi-gija*), the "parasitic press" (*gisaeng-eonron*), or the "slave-like press" (*buyeok-eonron*). They also positively assert that these journalists accept "pocket money" (*yongdon*) from powerful institutions. In particular, "accepting pocket money" is often described as "a major means of a *giraegi*'s livelihood."

Second, unethical behaviors of journalists are described as *giraegi*-like behaviors. The use and modification of a copyrighted work in a news story without permission from the copyright owner is a crucial example. To call out and mock this unethical *giraegi*-like behavior, one anonymous Korean created Twitter and Tumblr accounts, @giregi_giregi and giregi (giregi. tumblr.com), respectively. This anti-*giraegi* Twitter account @giregi_giregi aims to "permanently preserve embarrassing news stories by capturing and preserving them on online." On the Tumblr achieve, what is called "*giraegi* collection," @giregi_giregi has also "collected" the cases of the "absurd, unethical journalistic practices." On March 2, 2015, for example, @giregi_ giregi posted a captured screen shot showing that a reporter of *The Korea Economic Daily* had illegally used and transformed a photo copyrighted by another news medium Bloter.com.

In addition, reporters who do not treat the victims of a tragedy with dignity and sensitivity are considered unethical and unprofessional and therefore called *giraegi*s. During the rescue operation of the Sewol ferry tragedy, in particular, many inexperienced reporters competitively attempted to conduct intrusive interviews with the victims' family members and friends dealing with extraordinary grief (Um, 2014). Further, for the purpose of increasing Web traffic, the executives of some news outlets even ordered their news staff to create attention-grabbing stories using such keywords as "the Sewol ferry disaster," "sinking," and "tragedy." As a result, one online news outlet posted a news story introducing disaster films, such as *Titanic* (1997) and *Poseidon (*2006), with a click-bait headline containing the phrase "the Sewol ferry disaster" (Jo, 2014).

Third, Koreans identify a journalist as a *giraegi* when the journalist does not put enough effort into verifying unsubstantiated material. A crucial example is to exactly duplicate either the news reports provided by a news agency or press releases. In some cases, news stories published by multiple news media have exactly the same typos because all of them were just copied from a report provided by a news agency that initially made the typos.[7] In addition, the "he said, she said" style of reporting is often considered a *giraegi*-like journalistic practice. By relying on quotations from sources,

7   To see some examples of this stenographic practice of Korean journalists, visit the Tumblr page "*giraegi* collection" (http://giregi.tumblr.com; accessed on March 10, 2015).

especially powerful institutions, journalists seem to evade their responsibility to investigate the veracity of the news story. This was particularly true when most news media gave the wrong information about the number of rescued passengers who were on the Sewol ferry on April 16, 2014. Virtually every mainstream news outlet, including national broadcasting networks and news agency, relied on the information provided by the government spokesman briefing that every passenger would be safely rescued. However, this information was later found to be inaccurate. This error collectively made by Korean journalists is considered one of the crucial factors causing a serious delay in the rescue operation and thereby mass casualties.

In the same vein, those reporters who do not provide appropriate sources for their information and especially plagiarize another's work—such as academic papers, foreign news stories, and blogs—are also labeled as *giraegi*s. In other words, people criticize a lack of originality and of transparency in a news story, as expressed in the following tweet: "This *giraegi* should be ashamed of his garbage-like news story. I am sure that this garbage is simply copied from a Japanese news story I read before word for word." In particular, news stories using multiple unnamed sources found online have been severely criticized. For example, many news stories about the personal lives or conduct of celebrities, television shows, or any kind of gossip tend to begin with such phrases as "Recently, netizens (*nurikkun*) talk about XXX . . ." and then end with a series of references to comments, posts, or tweets posted by multiple anonymous netizens. In this case, reporters are barely transparent about and original in their investigative processes. Therefore, it is not easy to know how the reporters knew what they knew, who the sources were, and whether the reporters added anything that did not happen. Further, many reporters who produce this type of news stories do not disclose their names and e-mail addresses in their news stories.

In order to ridicule these reporters, Korean web developer Lee Junghaeng, called @rainygirl, developed the bot "*giraegi* button" performing a routine task to create a *giraegi*-like news story. A single click on the *giraegi* button, provided on an online community called *Daily Worst (ilgan-woseuteu*; ilwar. com), automatically produces a *giraegi*-like news story about any post produced by *Daily Worst* members.[8] The members of *Daily Worst* pejoratively define a journalist as "a person employed to compose fake reactions of netizens to popular search trends and then to write a story based on these fake reactions." In a notice about the *giraegi* button, the members of *Daily Worst* also suggest that "journalists who are enthusiastically monitoring our community are welcome to use the *giraegi* button. . . . The *giraegi* button will automatically produce the netizens' reactions for you" (*Daily Worst*, 2014). In short, by satirically imitating the reporters' practices, these Koreans request reporters to be transparent in terms of their sources and methods and also to rely on their own original reporting.

Lastly, a reporter using a click-bait headline (*naksi-geul*) is identified as a *giraegi*. This click-bait headline is carefully crafted to create a "curiosity gap." According to Derek Thompson (2013) from *The Atlantic*, "The idea is both to share just enough [so] that readers know what they're clicking and to withhold just enough to compel the click." Many Korean Twitter users share links to those news stories making them click and then mock the reporters who wrote the news stories. For example, tweets like "Indeed, #*giraegi* is in his office right now. Another click-bait headline is detected!," "Wow! Look at this #*giraegi*'s wonderful creativity!," and "I really wonder how much money this #*giraegi* earn by writing this garbage" are quite aggressive statements expressing anger toward the click-bait headlines, like "You Won't Believe What Happened in Seoul Now" and "Car Insurance Companies Hate This New Trick." The anti-*giraegi* Twitter account @giregi_giregi is also collecting samples of click-bait headlines. In an interview with an independent news startup called *Slow News* (Jinhyeok Lee, 2014), @giregi_giregi said, "Twitter and Tumblr users keep sending messages to me to inform me about wrongdoing by journalists. Further, finding click-bait

8 For the detailed information about the "*giraegi* button," visit https://github.com/rainy girl/giregi or http://ilwar.com/notice/172108 (accessed on March 10, 2015). In addition, in the United States, there is a similar kind of bot called "clickbait headline generator." This bot performs a routine task generating such headlines as "51 Lies Some Northerners Won't Believe Actually Exist." To explore this bot, visit http://community.usvsth3m.com/ generator/clickbait-headline-generator (accessed on March 10, 2015).

headlines is an effortless task because there are too many cases." "@giregi_
giregi has continued to amass followers," @giregi_giregi continued, "This is
a sign that Koreans are increasingly irritated by Korean news media, especially the click-bait culture."

In sum, these four patterns of the behaviors of Korean journalists—
namely, being loyal to power-holders, practicing unethical behaviors, lacking
originality and transparency, and creating the click-bait culture—contribute
to the emergence and consolidation of the discourse of *giraegi*. These *giraegi*-
like journalistic practices can be seen as the products of the instrumental
view of journalism that has been developed and maintained in the Korean
journalistic culture. The media corporations, for example, impose a "click-
bait mentality" on their news staff due to profit demands caused by the
decrease in advertising (Um, 2014). In this situation, by the socialization
mechanisms such as the *seonbae-hubae* system, *yama* practice, and the press
club system (Shin, 2016a), the news staff can internalize the "click-bait
mentality" and start to use page views as a key measure of journalistic
success. This hybrid of journalistic standard inevitably leads to sacrificing the
quality of news stories provided to the public.

The discourse of *giraegi* is an active reaction of Korean citizens to this
instrumentalization of Korean journalism. In other words, the emergence of
this discourse of *giraegi* reflects how much Koreans care about journalism
issues. In particular, the offensive nature in the discourse of *giraegi* reveals
how much Koreans are disappointed by Korean journalism. The discourse of
giraegi is powerful enough to impose a certain meaning and coherence on
various journalists' practices. Putting it differently, when Koreans evaluate
the quality of journalism and share their opinions about it, they now have a
modifier, "*giraegi*-like," to describe any kind of wrongdoing by Korean
journalists. Using the term *giraegi* to identify journalists enables a critical
part of Koreans to immediately understand and predict the nature of the
journalists' news stories.

The discourse of *giraegi* influences the symbolic boundaries (Abbott,
1988) of Korean journalism. The emergence of the discourse of *giraegi* leads
Korean journalists to reconsider their roles in Korean society. The discourse

of *giraegi* influences the emergence of metajournalistic discourse in the Korean journalistic community, attempts by journalists to evaluate, negotiate, and/or defend their own significance in society. In 2014, for example, some younger journalists publicly apologized for their conduct during the Sewol ferry tradegy, confessing "We were *giraegis*" (e.g., The KBS Union of Media Workers, 2014; Um, 2014). Meanwhile, other journalists, for instance, KBS Digital News director Sung Changgyeong, responded to these public apologies, arguing that the younger journalists who had apologized may have been "instigated by the leftist union executives" (Hyosil Kim, 2015). These journalists' reactions to the discourse of *giraegi* may in turn compete with each other to define what Korean journalism should be in Korean society.

The discourse of *giraegi* ultimately functions as "a shock to the [Korean journalism] system" (Ryfe, 2006: 141), causing a renegotiation of who a journalist is and what are considered good journalistic behaviors. Along with this shock, there has been another shock to the Korean journalistic culture. In particular, this has come from *inside* the journalistic community: *Nonprofit, citizen funded journalism.*

A GOOD JOURNALISM: NONPROFIT, CITIZEN FUNDED JOURNALISM

While a large segment of Korean society has sought to challenge the dominant culture of the journalistic community, a new model of journalism has been in the spotlight due to its possibility of filling the void left by the absence of *good journalism* in Korean society—nonprofit, citizen-funded journalism. At the end of 2014 and the beginning of 2015, several media critics published reports on the performance of Korean journalists in 2014, especially during the Sewol ferry tragedy, criticizing their unprofessional performance and introducing the emergence of the discourse of *giraegi* (e.g., Sewok Kim, 2014b). At the same time, these media critics emphasized the increasing public attention toward the performance of several digitally native news nonprofits, such as *GoBalNews* and *Newstapa.* These news nonprofits were established during the Lee Myung-bak administration by small groups of veteran journalists who had been fired or voluntarily resigned from the mainstream news media. These news nonprofits aim to "expose abuses of power by political elites and business leaders . . . [and] become the voices of the voiceless who are ignored by the mainstream news media" (*GoBalNews*, 2012). They also seek to "challenge routinized or institutionalized ways of journalism in the mainstream news media . . . [and ultimately] revitalize the dying Korean journalism" (*Newstapa*, 2012). In terms of journalistic method, these news nonprofits emphasize the significance of "the moral force of *investigative reporting* in the public interest" (*Newstapa*, 2012; italics added).

These news nonprofits receive funding from individual citizens. Since each of the news nonprofits were established in 2012, the number of donors has steadily increased. For example, the investigative news startup *Newstapa* started to raise donations on July 6, 2012. In less than ten days, around 2,200 citizens signed up to be a donor and decided to make a monthly donation, at least KRW 10,000 (approximately USD 10) to sponsor *Newstapa*. The number of donors has continued to grow, and by April 2016, they amounted to around 36,100. According to *Newstapa* president Youngjin Kim, "the financial soundness of *Newstapa* is strong enough to run *Newstapa*. Compared to the business model of other newly established TV stations and online news media that relies on advertising revenue, *Newstapa* model has achieved greater financial sustainability" (personal communication, September 30, 2014). This business model funded solely by individual citizens is different from that of other nonprofit news organizations in other countries that are funded mostly by large foundations or international nongovernmental organizations, such as the Knight Foundation and Open Society Foundations (Konieczna & Robinson, 2014; Requejo-Alemán & Lugo-Ocando, 2014).

The sustainability of this distinct funding model of Korean news nonprofits shows how much those Koreans who care about journalism look forward to the performance of these news nonprofits. These Koreans rely on the news nonprofits for much of their political information. They argue that the news nonprofits deserve support because they are much more credible and trusted news source than the mainstream news media and consequently contribute to the democratic development of Korea (Jo, 2012). On social networking sites, it is easy to find the posts expressing support for the news nonprofits, as found in tweets like "#*Newstapa* and #*GoBalNews* are the last bastion of Korean journalism. I hope that my donation will help them to continue to be a beacon for ordinary people like me," "The truth will always be revealed by @*Newstapa*, @*GObalnews*, and @*sisapapais*," "In the current situation in which the quality of journalism is below minimum standard, the number of the donors of the true news organization @*Newstapa* should grow to 100,000," and "I increase the monthly donation amount for #*Newstapa*. Why? *Newstapa* staff put every effort into producing 'real' news! :-)" In particular, a contraposition between the mainstream news media and news nonprofits is a noticeable pattern in the posts published by the supporters of the nonprofit news organizations, as seen in such tweets as: "Listen *giraegi*s! You may not have produced this kind of garbage http://t.co/cBYKRYc4Zk, if you had watched the special issue of #Newstapa published in the early of 2015. Watch this: http://newstapa.org/22775" and "Agreed, @MBC_PDChoi. The mainstream news media, especially the Chosun jjirasi,[9] that routinely distort facts are shams! I am no longer patient with their intolerable *giraegi*-like news. Go for it, #Newstapa and #GObalnews! You are my havens!"

The quality of the news nonprofits' work is also acknowledged by many journalism awards. Between 2012 and 2014, the journalists of *Newstapa* were awarded 25 prestigious journalism awards, including the Ahn Jong-phil Prize for Press Freedom, the Song-Geon-ho Prize, and the Lee Young-hee Prize. In addition, in 2014, *GoBalNews* journalist Lee Sangho was also awarded several professional awards, including the Democratic Journalism Award and the Truthful Journalism Award. As one of the jurors of the 2014 Democratic Journalism Award said, the journalists of these news nonprofits "are awarded because they re-connect Koreans with the most important

---

9 "*Jjirasi*" refers to any document containing rumors and gossip. This term originates from unpublished documents containing business information about companies' prospects circulating around the Korean securities market.

news about public affairs, . . . which have been missed by mainstream journalists" (Sewok Kim, 2014a). At the award ceremony for the Ahn-Jong-phil
Prize on October 24, 2012, Moon Young-hee, the president of the Ahn
Jong-Phil Prize as well as a former journalist who had fought for press
freedom during the military regimes in the 1970s and the 1980s, also said,
"We don't need the mainstream news media, such as the *KBS* and the *MBC*,
anymore because we now have the news nonprofits, especially *Newstapa*" (Jo,
2012).

In short, the exploratory project of the news nonprofits is the process of
contesting the conventional logic of Korean journalism—especially the
instrumental view of journalism and the *giraegi*-like journalistic practices—
and thereby reestablishing the professional boundaries of the Korean journalistic culture. The news nonprofits are challenging and denying the privi-
leged position of the mainstream news media in Korean society. In the
current situation in which the majority of Korean journalists are treated
without respect, the emerging model of journalism that the news nonprofits
are practicing seems to serve as an engine driving constitutive choices (Starr,
2004) for the Korean journalistic culture. The challenge of the news nonprofits to the dominant logic of journalism is a process of setting a new
evaluation criterion for the performance of Korean journalists.

References

Amnesty International. (2009, March 25). Journalist detained since Sunday in South Korea. Retrieved March 5, 2015, from http://www.refworld.org/docid/49cb32dbc.html

Choe, S. (2011, November 1). By lampooning leaders, talk show channels young people's anger. *The New York Times*. Retrieved from http://www.nytimes.com/2011/11/02/world/asia/lampooning-leaders-talk-show-channels-young-peoples-anger-in-south-korea.html?pagewanted=1&_r=0&emc=eta1

——— (2012, April 9). Spying Scandal Is Called South Korea's Watergate. *The New York Times*. Retrieved from http://www.nytimes.com/2012/04/10/world/asia/government-spying-charges-complicate-korean-vote.html

Choi, J.-Y. (2012). South Korean Broadcasters Keep Up Strike for Media Independence. *Los Angeles Times*. Retrieved from http://articles.latimes.com/2012/jul/10/world/la-fg-korea-media-strike-20120711

Choi, S., & Jie, S. (2014). *Offer Vocie to the Voiceless, Not Power: An Interview with Newstapa Producer Seungho Choi*. Seoul, Korea: Cheolsuwayeonghui.

Daily Worst. (2014, October 8). Add Giraegi Button. Retrieved March 10, 2015, from http://ilwar.com/notice/172108

Fairclough, G. (2004). Generation why?: The 386ers of Korea Question Old Rules. *The Wall Street Journal*. Retrieved from http://online.wsj.com/article/0,,SB108189445695281806,00.html

Freedom House. (2011). *Freedom of the Press 2011: South Korea* (Online). Retrieved from http://www.freedomhouse.org/report/freedom-press/2011/south-korea

Friedhoff, K. (2014, May 15). Ferry crisis strikes heavy blow to public trust. *The Wall Street Journal*. Retrieved from http://blogs.wsj.com/korearealtime/2014/05/15/ferry-crisis-strikes-heavy-blow-to-public-trust/

GoBalNews. (2012). The introduction of GoBalNews. *GoBalNews*. Retrieved March 16, 2015, from http://www.gobalnews.com/com/com-1.html

International Federation of Journalists. (2009, March 31). South Korean authorities must release journalists' leader, says IFJ. Retrieved March 5, 2015, from http%3A%2F%2Fwww.ifj.org%2Fnc%2Fnews-single-view%2Fcategory%2Fevents-1%2Farticle%2Fsouth-korean-authorities-must-release-journalists-leader-says-ifj%2F

Jeong, Y. (2011). *The record of Jeong Yeonju: From the Dong-A Struggle Committee to President Roh Moo-hyun*. Paju, Korea: Yurichang.

Jie, S., & Lee, S. (2012). *Lee Sangho's GoBal News*. Seoul, Korea: Dongasia.

Jo, H. (2011, November 27). Expelled MBC reporters. *Media Today*. Retrieved from http://www.mediatoday.co.kr/news/articleView.html?idxno=98733

Jo, S.-K. (2012, October 25). We Don't Need the KBS and the MBC Because We Have the Newstapa. *Media Today*. Retrieved from http://www.mediatoday.co.kr/news/articleView.html?idxno=105719

Jo, Y. (2014, April 19). An excuse for giraegis. *Media Today*. Retrieved from http://m.media

today.co.kr/news/articleView.html?idxno=116082

Jung, Y.-I. (2012, April 21). Is the "Naggomsu" Possible to Play a Pivotal Role in the Presidential Campaign? *The Kyunghyang Shinmun.* Retrieved from http://news.khan. co.kr/kh_news/khan_art_view.html?artid=201204211057241&code=910100

Kim, H. (2015, May 9). The KBS Digital News Director Sung says, "Stop Instigating the News Staff." *The Hankyoreh.* Retrieved from http://www.hani.co.kr/arti/society/soci ety_general/636230.html

Kim, S. (2014a, December 16). Newstapa and JTBC dominate awards list. *PD Journal.* Retrieved from http://www.pdjournal.com/news/articleView.html?idxno=54070

_____ (2014b, December 29). Giraegi journalism. *PD Journal.* Retrieved from http:// www.pdjournal.com/news/articleView.html?idxno=54168

Kim, W. (2013, April 4). News Companies Seem to Want to Maintain Giraegi System. *Mediaus.* Retrieved from http://www.mediaus.co.kr/news/articleView.html?idxno=33 180

Konieczna, M., & Robinson, S. (2014). Emerging News Non-Profits: A Case Study for Rebuilding Community Trust? *Journalism,* 15(8): 968–986. http://doi.org/10.1177/146 4884913505997

La Rue, Frank. (2011). *Report of the Special Rapporteur on the Promotion and Protection of the Right to Freedom of Opinion and Expression, Frank La Rue* (No. A/HRC/17/27/Add.2). Geneva, Switzerland: Office of the United Nations High Commissioner for Human Rights. Retrieved from http://www.humanrights.asia/news/ahrc-news/AHRC-STM-155-2008/?searchterm

Lee, J. (1997). Press freedom and democratization: South Korea's experience and some lessons. *International Communication Gazette,* 59(2): 135–149. http://doi.org/10.1177/ 0016549297059002004

_____ (2014, December 26). Giraegi Collection: Reporters, Don't Cross That River. *Slow News.* Retrieved from http://slownews.kr/35380

_____ (2015, February 2). The KCC Hands Off the Reformation of the Structure of the Public Broadcasting System. *The Hankyoreh.* Retrieved from http://www.hani.co.kr/ arti/society/media/676474.html

Lee, K. (2003). Pressures for Media Reform in Korea: There are Loud Calls for Changes in the Way the Press and Government Interact. *Nieman Reports,* 57(4): 93–95.

Merrill, J. C. (1993). *The Dialectic in Journalism: Toward a Responsible Use of Press Freedom.* Baton Rouge, LA: Louisiana State University Press.

Nam, I. (2014, May 16). Media Outlets Apologize over Sewol ferry Disaster Coverage. *The Wall Street Journal.* Retrieved from http://blogs.wsj.com/korearealtime/2014/05/16/ media-outlets-apologize-over-sewol-ferry-disaster-coverage/

Newstapa. (2012, March 31). The Illegal Surveillance of Private Citizens III. *Newstapa.* Retrieved from http://newstapa.org/221

Park, S. (2014). *Everything Happened by Chance, and Then Here I Am.* Paju, Korea: Pureunsup.

Requejo-Alemán, J. L., & Lugo-Ocando, J. (2014). Assessing the sustainability of Latin American investigative non-profit journalism. *Journalism Studies*, 15(5): 522–532. http://doi.org/10.1080/1461670X.2014.885269

Rhee, J. W., & Kim, E.-M. (2012). Democratization and the Changing Media Environment in South Korea. In H. A. Semetko & M. Scammell (eds.). *The SAGE Handbook of Political Communication* (pp. 415–426). Thousand Oaks, CA: Sage Publications.

Roh, J.-M. (2012). *Roh Jong-Myun's Breakthrough*. Seoul, Korea: Purple Cow.

Ryfe, D. M. (2006). Guest Editor's Introduction: New Institutionalism and the News. *Political Communication*, 23(2): 135–144.

Shin, W. (2016a). Being a "Truth-Teller" in the Unsettled Period of Korean Journalism: A Case Study of Newstapa and its Boundary Work (Doctoral dissertation, University of Minnesota).

_____ (2016b). Conservative Journalists' Myth Making in South Korea: Use of the Past in News Coverage of the 2008 Korean Candlelight Vigil. *Asian Studies Review*, 40(1): 120–136. http://doi.org/10.1080/10357823.2015.1126221

Starr, P. (2004). *The Creation of the Media: Political Origins of Modern Communications*. New York, NY: Basic Books.

Swidler, A. (1986). Culture in action: Symbols and strategies. *American Sociological Review*, 51(2): 273–286.

Thompson, D. (2013, November 14). Upworthy: I Thought This Website Was Crazy, But What Happened Next Changed Everything. *The Atlantic*. Retrieved from http://www.theatlantic.com/business/archive/2013/11/upworthy-i-thought-this-website-was-crazy-but-what-happened-next-changed-everything/281472/

Um, J. (2014, May 20). Four journalists reporting the Sewol Ferry disaster said, "We were Giraegis." *The Hankyoreh 21*. Retrieved from http://www.hani.co.kr/arti/society/society_general/637999.html

Partisan Media and Polarized Opinion in South Korea

A Review

3

JIYOUNG HAN

Communication Media Research Center,
Ewha Woman's University

An absolute majority of Korean voters (91.6%) is concerned about the growing polarization in their country (Korean Center for Social Conflict Resolution & Hankook Research, 2017; see also Yoon, 2015). They find the split along ideological lines as critical a problem facing the nation as the polarization of wealth. This report also identifies the National Assembly and the press as the top two actors most responsible for the current political milieu. Indeed, research has uncovered a wider ideological gap among partisan elites (Kang, 2014; Lee, 2011; Park & Kim, 2016). For the last two decades, Korean journalism has been notorious for its partisan slant (Lee, 2008; Lee & Lee, 2016; Park & Kim, 2016; Nam, 2009).

However polarized political elites may be, such ideological polarization has not been transmitted to the Korean mass public (Lee, 2009; Lee, 2011; see Kim, 2015b for a counter arguement). From 2002 to 2012, whereas the ideological split among the members of the National Assembly widened— from 1.7 to 3.2—the ideological gap among the general population re- mained largely the same, if not falling a little—from 2.95 to 2.40 (Kang, Ha, Kim & Kwan, 2014). Nonetheless, public opinion polls persistently show a clear division along party lines on various social issues and candidate preferences (Kim, 2015b; Lee, 2011).

A very similar phenomenon has been observed in the United States, where bipartisanship characterizes the country's politics. A considerable section of the American electorate locates itself at the center of an ideological continuum (Fiorina & Abrams, 2008; see Abramowitz, 2010 for evidence showing the polarized mass public) while rivalry between the two major parties in Congress has become more vigorous (Druckman, Peterson, & Slothuus, 2013; Pew Research Center, 2013). Researchers argue that polarized partisan elites ultimately guide mass polarization. When partisan elites, most apparently elected officers, send out divergent issue positions, citizens are aligned with the positions of their political parties and in turn public opinion emerges as being polarized along party lines. This phenomenon is conceptualized as *partisan sorting* (Fiorina & Abrams, 2008; Layman, Carsey, Green, Herrera, & Cooperma, 2010; Levendusky, 2009) and ample evidence of such influence of elite cues on polarization has been documented (e.g., Cohen, 2003; Layman, Carsey, Green, Herrera, & Cooperma, 2010; Nicholson, 2012).

What is understudied in this process of mass polarization is the role of mass media (Han & Federico, in press). For example, Druckman and colleagues (2013) showed that the polarizing effect of elite polarization cues abated as the level of elite polarization in Congress was described as less "stark" in news coverage of political events. Slothuus and de Vreese (2010) found no polarization among participants reading news coverage of partisan consensus on trade issues; but participants reading a news story on partisan conflict on a welfare policy were polarized along party lines. These prior findings build on an assumption that media mirror political reality as it is and thus there is not much room for discussing independent roles of media in addition to partisan elite cues.

A whole host of media studies suggest otherwise, however. First, media oversell political conflict in their news coverage (Aalberg, Stromback, & de Vreese, 2012; Cappella & Jamieson, 1997; de Vreese, 2012; Dekavalla, 2016; Dunaway & Lawrence, 2015; Patterson, 1993; Schmuck, Heiss, Matthes, Engesser, & Esser, 2017). According to Levendusky and Malhotra (2016), media emphasis on partisan conflict fosters an exaggerated sense of polarization in the minds of news consumers. More studies have begun to report that when media overplay partisan conflicts in their news coverage, news consumers express polarized positions on the issue in the news story (Han & Federico, 2017; Han & Wackman, 2017; see also van Klingeren, Boomgaarden, & de Vreese, 2017).

Second, the rise of partisan cable news channels (e.g., *Fox News* and *MSNBC*) amplifies partisan arguments and increases user selectivity (Bennett & Iyengar, 2008; Iyengar & Hahn, 2009; Stroud, 2008). Copious research finds that news consumers selectively tune in to news channels resonating with their political viewpoints—i.e., Republicans watch *Fox News* or Democrats watch *MSNBC*—and this congenial news exposure reinforces prior attitudes and in turn contributes to greater polarization (Arceneaux & Johnson, 2014; Arceneaux, Johnson, & Cryderman, 2013; Bennett & Iyengar, 2008; Hollander, 2008; Iyengar & Hahn, 2009; Jones, 2002; Levendusky, 2013; Stroud, 2008, 2010). Furthermore, partisans are also accidentally or purposefully exposed to news channels that challenge their political perspectives (Gentzkow & Shapiro, 2011; Pew Research Center, 2014; see Prior, 2013 for a review). Some studies found that uncongenial news exposure as such—i.e., Republicans watching *MSNBC* or Democrats watching *Fox News*—produces an even greater impact on polarization relative to congenial news exposure (Arceneaux et al., 2013; Levendusky, 2013; Lodge & Taber, 2013; Slothuus & de Vreese, 2010).

An emphasis on partisan conflict and an apparent political slant are also features of the Korean press. Particularly, Korean news outlets are sharply divided along ideological lines (Lee, 2008; Rhee & Choi, 2005; Shin & Lee, 2014; Nam, 2009). Numerous studies have revealed a wide array of public issues—e.g., nuclear energy (Choi, 2016), North Korea-related diplomacy (Hong & Son, 2017; Kim, 2015), real estate holding tax (Choi, 2010), and the Sewol Ferry disaster (Kim, Ham, & Kim, 2017; Park, 2016)—framed differently in conservative versus progressive news media. Politically biased news stories also tend to highlight partisan conflict (Han & Wackman, 2017; Levendusky, 2013). Korean news media have long been lambasted for their level of attention to partisan conflict without presenting background information or deeper analyses on the causes of the conflict (Choi, 2014; J. Lee, 2008).

What is different between Korean and American news media, however, is that a political bias in news coverage is not limited to cable news channels in Korea. Even public broadcasters, namely, *Korean Broadcasting System* (*KBS*) and *Munhwa Broadcasting Corporation* (*MBC*), which take up much of prime time viewership are accused of being biased toward conservatives as well (Choi, 2014; Kim & Park, 2010; Park & Chang, 2000). In addition, the top three newspapers (the *Chosun Ilbo, Joongang Ilbo,* and *Dong-A Ilbo*), which together take up more than fifty percent of readership (Choi, 2003; Lee, 2008), also present an overtly conservative slant in their news coverage (Kim, 2011).

In the United States, on the other hand, despite the growing popularity of partisan cable news channels, the average viewership of the three non-partisan networks (i.e., *NBC, CBS,* and *ABC*) remains more than twenty times larger than that of the top three partisan cable channels (i.e., *Fox News, MSNBC,* and *CNN*; Pew Research Center, 2014). In summary, whereas the majority of Americans still consumes non-partisan news stories, Koreans are in general exposed to politically biased news that is mostly in favor of conservatives (Choi, 2003; Hahn, Park, Lee, & Lee, 2013; Lee, 2015; Min & Lee, 2015; Shin & Lee, 2014).

This paper reviews studies testing how such characteristics of the Korean news media are associated with the growing partisan issue polarization among the Korean mass public. This paper then reviews three theories that current research suggests as explanations for the link between news exposure and political attitude polarization. I also review how these research trends are adopted in Korea. To conclude, unique research trends on related topics in Korea are discussed in light of its limitations and future opportunities.

Selective News Exposure and Political Polarization

The prominence of the media's political biases in its news coverage has prompted Korean media scholars to investigate ideological selectivity in media use. There is much supporting evidence. According to Korea Press Foundation's (2016) survey of 5,128 Korean adults, the readership of conservative newspapers (e.g., the *Chosun Ilbo*) includes more conservatives (47.3% vs. 22.5% liberals) while the opposite (20.0% conservatives vs. 55.0% liberals) is true in the case of progressive newspapers (e.g., the *Hankyoreh Shinmun*; see also Min & Lee, 2015). A similar pattern is found with regard to the viewership of public broadcasters, *MBC* and *KBS*. They are known as to be biased toward conservatives (Choi, 2014; Kim & Park, 2010; Park & Chang, 2000); their viewership consists of about 40% conservatives and less than 25 % liberals.

Such a tendency of selective exposure congenial to individuals' political ideology appears to be more prominent on social network sites (SNSs) such as Kakao Story, Facebook, and Twitter (Park, 2014; Roh & Min, 2012; Hwang, 2013). Hahn and colleagues' (2013) analyses on individual Twitter users' followership of the 111th U.S. Senate and the 18th Korean National Assembly show that Korean Twitter users in particular build homogeneous networks and are barely exposed to opposing political arguments. Moreover, Korean Twitter users are more polarized along ideological lines than their political elites.

Relatedly, it is important to note that Korean liberals and conservatives exhibit a diverging pattern in their media use. Whereas conservatives tend to rely on traditional news media (e.g., television and newspapers), liberals more frequently consume news online (Kim & Son, 2015; Korea Press Foundation, 2016). Based on Lee's (2014) study, only 18.4% of conservatives indicated Internet and news portals as their primary sources of daily news. The corresponding statistic doubled in the case of liberals (38.0%). This difference is in part related to the fact that the mainstream news media in Korea largely leans toward conservatives (Choi, 2003; Hahn et al., 2013; Lee, 2015; Min & Lee, 2015; Shin & Lee, 2014). In this vein, some research finds a stronger tendency of selective partisan exposure among liberals, who are actively looking for alternative news sources other than traditional media (Lee, 2014; Roh & Min, 2012).

One political consequence of congenial news exposure is attitude polarization—liberals tuning in to liberal media and conservatives tuning in to conservative media are further apart in their expression of positions on contentious social issues (Arceneaux & Johnson, 2014; Arceneaux et al., 2013; Bennett & Iyengar, 2008; Hollander, 2008; Iyengar & Hahn, 2009; Jones, 2002; Levendusky, 2013; Stroud, 2008, 2010). This polarizing effect of selective partisan exposure is supported in Korea (Lee & Cho, 2017; Min, 2016b; Park, 2014; Roh & Min, 2012). Son (2004) found that the use of progressive media such as the *Hankyoreh Shinmun* and *OhmyNews*, an Internet-based news service, forecast participants' amicable positions on North Korea-related issues; in contrast, the use of conservative dailies such as the *Chosun Ilbo* and *Dong-A Ilbo* reinforced participants' hostile attitudes toward these issues (see also Jhee et al., 2013). Min (2016) also found that selective exposure to likeminded news sources was positively correlated with polarized attitudes toward political parties and their candidates in the congressional by-elections.

Although the magnitude of the positive relationship between selective exposure and attitude polarization did not differ between liberals and conservatives in Min's (2016) study, there is research showing ideological asymmetry as well. Specifically, in the 2014 Seoul mayoral election, progressive newspapers and SNSs intensified the biases of the supporters of the liberal party; however, this was not true of conservative newspapers and SNSs (Lee, 2014; see also Park, 2014; Roh & Min, 2012). With regard to a greater influence of partisan selective exposure on attitude polarization among liberal relative to conservatives, Lee (2014) sheds light on liberals' motivation to actively search for supporting information online. That is, given the prevalence of a conservative bias in mainstream news media, liberals avoid using traditional media that often, if not always, challenge their political beliefs and values, and display an intense need for alternative news sources that would resonate with their political worldviews. Moreover, liberals, who take an advantage of increasing selectivity in the era of digital media and consume progressive news stories online are more politically engaged and have a greater interest in politics. Liberals' exposure to likeminded news stories therefore is likely to induce greater attitude polarization relative to conservatives' partisan selective exposure (Roh & Min, 2012).

Despite wide support for users' preferences for congenial news sources over uncongenial ones, refuting evidence is also present. First, with the analyses of an actual log-data on access to Internet news sites, Shin and Lee (2014) demonstrated no significant difference along ideological lines in the actual use of online newspaper websites, including both conservative (the *Chosun Ilbo, Joongang Ilbo,* and *Dong-A Ilbo*) and progressives ones (the *Hankyoreh Shinmun* and *Kyunghyang Shinmun*; see also Min & Lee, 2015). Second, in Choi and Lee's (2012) experimental study, participants did not show a distinct preference for positive news stories over negative ones with respect to their preformed attitudes toward the given issue (i.e., about the Korea-U.S. Free Trade Agreement (FTA)). After news selection, moreover, both strong supporters and opponents relieved their strong opinions on the FTA without hesitation (see also Cho & Cho, 2013).

Mixed support for selective partisan exposure and its consequence of attitude polarization is not unique to Korea. In the United States, Gentzkow and Shapiro (2011) also found weak evidence for partisan selectivity in online media use. By examining Internet tracking data, they revealed that most of the largest news websites (e.g., www.nytimes.com, www.huffington post.com, and www.foxnews.com) attracted a similar amount of traffic from conservative, moderate, and liberal users. By contrast, studies of selective exposure on cable news channels found strong evidence of ideological segregation in Americans' media use (Coe et al., 2008; Hollander, 2008; Stroud, 2010): Republicans and conservatives reported more exposure to conservative outlets, whereas Democrats and liberals reported greater exposure to liberal sources. Taken together, Prior's (2013) meta-analysis concluded that there is no consensus to date for the polarizing effect of selective partisan media exposure. Therefore, researchers have recently begun to pay more attention to under what conditions and/or through what mechanisms news exposure leads to political polarization among the mass public.

MECHANISMS BEHIND THE POLARIZING EFFECT OF NEWS EXPOSURE

Current literature proposes three theoretical mechanisms that delineate how news exposure generates political polarization: motivated reasoning, inter-party animus, and self-stereotyping. Below, each of these three theoretical approaches is reviewed along with its application to Korean media research on the given topic.

Defensive Motivated Reasoning

Congenial exposure to an individual's political ideology reinforces partisans' prior attitudes, resulting in political attitude polarization (Bennett & Iyengar, 2008; Hollander, 2008; Iyengar & Hahn, 2009; Jones, 2002). Although partisans are also unexpectedly or purposefully exposed to news channels that challenge their political perspectives (Gentzkow & Shapiro, 2011; Pew Research Center, 2014), research finds that such uncongenial news exposure can generate even greater polarization (Arceneaux et al., 2013; Lodge & Taber, 2013; Slothuus & de Vreese, 2010). Taking Levendusky's (2013) study for example, conservative participants expressed greater support for the Bush tax cuts while liberals showed greater opposition to the issue after both likeminded and cross-cutting exposure to cable news channels—i.e., *Fox News* and *MSNBC*. Yet, the strongest polarization was observed among liberals and conservatives who experienced uncongenial news exposure and had strong prior attitudes, either positive or negative, toward tax cut issues (see also Druckman & Bolsen, 2011; Lodge & Taber, 2013). In other studies, such polarization following cross-cutting exposure is more pronounced among the more politically aware (Kahan, 2013; Lodge & Taber, 2013; Redlawsk, 2002; Slothuus & de Vreese, 2010).

This asymmetry on polarization following congenial or uncongenial exposure has been explained consistently with theories of motivated reasoning (Kunda, 1990). That is, people tend to process information in a way to confirm their preexisting attitudes and bolster them. In doing so, people evaluate arguments congenial to their beliefs as being more valid and persuasive while discrediting the quality of uncongenial arguments. Such biased information processing increases especially when individuals' beliefs and identities are threatened rather than encouraged (see Leeper & Slothuus, 2014 for a review). Evidence of attitude polarization along party lines as a result of defensive motivated reasoning has been corroborated in various contexts including candidate evaluation (Redlawsk, 2002), policy support (Druckman et al., 2013; Han & Federico, 2017; Hart & Nisbet, 2011; Levendusky, 2013; Lodge & Taber, 2013; Slothuus & de Vreese, 2010) and support for new technology (Druckman & Bolsen, 2011).

However, very little research in Korea has empirically tested the mediating role of defensive motivated reasoning in the process of news exposure leading toward political polarization. As an exception, Lee and Cho (2017) showed that partisan media use generated political attitude polarization via biased partisan interpretation. Although the authors do not adopt the term "motivated reasoning," their mediating variable of partisan interpretation was assessed by asking participants to what extent they agreed or disagreed with partisan arguments around the given topic; this is a measure that is used to gauge defensive motivated reasoning. Other research on uncongenial news exposure mostly explore its influences on knowledge learning (Choi & Lee, 2012; Min, 2016), political tolerance (e.g., Choi & Lee, 2012; Jang & Lee, 2010a, 2010b; Song, Shin, & Park, 2006), or political participation (e.g., Choi, 2015, 2016).

Instead of testing the hypothesis of defensive motivated reasoning, burgeoning literature suggests it as a reason why news consumers are easily misled by unverified information or fake news. For example, Roh, Choi, and Min (2017) found fake news acceptance during the 19th Presidential campaign in 2017 varied depending on whether the fake news coverage was negative or positive vis-à-vis the news consumers' favored candidate. To elaborate, respondents disproved fake news about their candidate but trusted fake news hostile to the opposing one (see also Lee, 2017). The authors speculate that the electorate's motivation to win an election fosters such a bias-perpetuating information processing.

Social Identity Theory and Intergroup Animus

The second mechanism behind the polarizing effect of news media is examined through a lens of social identity theory (SIT: Tajfel & Turner, 1979, 1986/2004). Copious evidence suggests that a mere ingroup/outgroup distinction is often sufficient to generate ingroup favoritism and outgroup derogation (Gaertner, Iuzzini, Witt, & Oriña, 2006; Otten & Mummendey, 2000). According to SIT, the primary cause of intergroup bias and discrimination is individuals' motivation to differentiate ingroup from outgroup in a positive light. On top of this basic motivation to evaluate the ingroup positively, a competitive social context can also encourage hostility toward outgroups.

These tendencies are evident in the two-party system of the United States. Using a panel data, Iyengar, Sood, and Lelkesn (2012) showed that over the course of the U.S. Presidential campaign in 2008 partisans evaluated their party more positively while expressing more hostile feelings toward the opposing party. This interparty animus was more pronounced in battleground states where intense negative campaigning was more prevalent. Beyond dislike, this interparty animus appears to spill over into biases in non-political judgments, such as decisions about the allocation of scholarships (Iyengar & Westwood, 2015). Iyengar, Sood, and Lelkes (2012) thus propose a shift of perspective in scholarly efforts to understand the growing political polarization in the United States from ideology to affect.

Unfortunately, in Korea no studies to date have analyzed political polarization with a particular focus on intergroup animus between conservatives and liberals. In an essay, however, Lee & Lee (2016) shed light on the ramifications of the political talk shows of *Channel A* and *TV Chosun* that galvanize strong negative emotions of anger and loathing toward progressive parties and pro-North Korea activists. They claim that such media-generated negative emotions targeted at opposing outgroups are detrimental to the future of Korean democracy. Future research may want to substantiate this conjecture consistent with social identity theory.

Self-categorization Theory and Partisan Self-stereotyping

In contrast to SIT of which tenets are ingroup favoritism and discrimination against outgroups, self-categorization theory (SCT: Turner, Hogg, Oakes, Reicher, & Wetherell, 1987) strictly centers on cognitive consequences of ingroup/outgroup differentiation. That is, according to SCT when an ingroup identity becomes salient as opposed to an outgroup identity (e.g., Democrats *versus* Republicans), people tend to assimilate their own attitudes and behaviors to those characteristic of the ingroup. This process, known as *self-stereotyping* (Hogg, 2003; Hogg & Turner, 1987), occurs on the basis of group prototypes—stereotypical attributes or defining features of groups (for empirical evidence see Cadinu & Galdi, 2012; Kuppens & Yzerbyt, 2012; Kuppens, Yzerbyt, Dandache, Fischer, & van der Schalk, 2013; Onorato & Turner, 2004). Group prototypes reflect a principle of *meta-contrast* (see also Oakes, 2002; Oakes, Turner, & Haslam, 1991; Turner, Oakes, Haslam, & McGarty, 1994). In essence, by inflating the differences between ingroups and outgroups while deflating the differences within groups, characteristics of ingroups and outgroups in comparison are both stereotypically exaggerated. Along these lines, prior research has shown that issue positions linked to a group prototype become more extreme when group members are informed that their group is in conflict with another (Mackie, 1986; Mackie & Cooper, 1984; Price, 1989).

This attitude polarization via self-stereotyping has been supported in political contexts as well. Han and Federico (2017) showed that after reading a news story about partisan conflict over a tax issue, Democrats and Republicans believed their party's issue stance to be more divergent from each other than it actually was and, in turn, their own attitudes toward the given issue became polarized in alignment with the perceived inparty position. In their experiment (Han and Federico's, 2017: Study 1), this mediating effect of partisan self-stereotyping toward polarization is persistent after controlling for that of partisan motivated reasoning (see also Han and Federico, in press). Similarly, Han and Wackman (2017) provide experimental evidence showing that partisan self-stereotyping is a different cognitive mechanism unpacking the news effect on polarization from partisan motivated reasoning.

Korean communication scholars adopt SCT more frequently than a motivated reasoning approach in an effort to advance their understanding of the media effect on mass political behaviors. However, Korean studies informed by SCT take a different tack than American ones inasmuch as they use SCT primarily to explain hostile media perception—a phenomenon in which people perceive neutral news reports on an intergroup conflict such as a war to be biased against their group (Vallone, Ross, & Lepper, 1985).

In conjunction with the fact that most Korean news outlets are not obscure in their political slant, Korean scholars have paid greater attention to explore how individuals' hostile media perception is altered by the presentation of news sources (Auh & Park, 2005; Hwang, 2007; Jhee et al., 2013; Kim, 2016; Kim, Lee, & Kim, 2016; Kim & Ha, 2014; Lee, 2015; see Reid, 2012 for an original theoretical discussion). For example, Song (2014) tested the changes in readers' perception on a neutral editorial depending on whether it was attributed to a conservative (the *Joongang Ilbo*) or progressive (the *Hankyoreh Shinmun*) newspaper. His results from an online experiment showed that without attribution readers found the news story unbiased. However, with an attribution to uncongenial media, readers indicated the news story as hostile to themselves while the opposite was true when the news story was attributed to congenial media. This effect of news source on the perception of media bias manifested as readers conceived stronger conservative or liberal political orientations (see also Kim, 2016; Kim et al., 2016; Lee, 2015).

Hostile media perception may invite individuals to take "corrective" actions to make their voices heard in the public sphere by actively attacking counterparts or promoting political activism (Choi, Park, & Chang, 2011; Rojas, 2010). In this vein, Kim (2016) showed that when individuals discerned media perpetuating political arguments opposing to their views, they expressed stronger intentions to sign a petition in a way to advocate their political beliefs. Importantly, they noted that this effect was mediated with a discrete emotion of anger. If the mediating variable here were not the discrete emotion of anger but group-based anger toward an outgroup (Kuppens et al., 2013; Mackie, Devos, & Smith, 2000) or an intergroup animus (Iyengar et al., 2012), Kim's (2016) study would be more relevant to SCT and SIT.

Likewise, Roh and Min's (2012) study offers another example, which is in need of theoretical sophistication. Although they hypothesized the polarizing effect of partisan selective exposure via increased political group identification, this mediating effect of political group identification was not supported. Informed by SCT, group identity salience does not directly induce attitude polarization but through a perceptually exaggerated ingroup prototype as opposed to that of outgroups. In the case of SIT, salient group identity triggers negative feelings toward outgroups and, in turn, polarization emerges. It would be great if the researchers tested the mediating role of partisan self-stereotyping or intergroup animus in addition to that of political group identity salience.

Conclusions: Limitations and Future Opportunities

In this review, I analyzed the current state of Korean research on the topic of media and polarization. Given that America makes a good real-world parallel to South Korea in terms of the political system led by two major parties and media portrayal of politics, I compared research trends in Korea to those in the United States. One critical difference between the two countries is that mainstream Korean news media are generally in favor of conservatives, whereas American news outlets, at least the three major networks (i.e., *NBC*, *CBS*, and *ABC*), are viewed as objective and non-partisan. This difference in media landscape leads Korean scholars to pay greater attention to the presence of selective partisan media exposure and its associated outcomes. As a result, an interesting asymmetry was found with respect to conservatives' and liberals' patterns in media use (Kim & Son, 2015; Korea Press Foundation, 2016; Lee, 2014).

Nonetheless, one limitation is the relative lack of scholarly effort in elucidating how exposure to congenial or uncongenial media induces political attitude polarization. Many Korean scholars point at blunt political biases in news media as a key factor in the growing polarization in contemporary Korean society. Identifying mechanisms behind this presumed relationship is imperative for encouraging scholars to further explore ways to combat this negative effect. However, there have been very few studies identifying such mechanisms and replicating the mediating role of defensive motivated reasoning, interparty animus, or partisan self-stereotyping in a theoretically rigorous manner. Paradoxically, this gap in the literature opens many doors for future research in Korea.

One interesting research question for future research lies in the fact that online news consumption frequently entails exposure to others' comments on a news story (Kim & Rhee, 2006; Kim & Sun, 2006). In considering that a significant portion of the comments are negative reactions to the news they are commenting on (Choi et al., 2016), it is worth noting that exposure to comments may provide challenging perspectives, which counterbalances the side effect of selective exposure to like-minded information. Research has supported the impact of others' comments posted under an online news story (Jang & Lee, 2010b; Lee & Jang, 2009; Yang, 2008). Moreover, Kang and Kim (2012) showed that after reading a politically neutral news story, participants inferred the general public opinion on a given issue from the comments and when the comments diverged from their own preferences, participants changed their issue stances in accordance with the comments. Such a tendency did not emerge on issues that participants found personally important (see also Lee, 2011). Defensive motivated reasoning may play a role in this moderating role of issue involvement.

Another future opportunity would be related to moderates who place themselves at the center of an ideological continuum (or Independents who support no political party in particular). In contrast to the United States where debates over the extent of mass polarization remain inconclusive,

Korean survey data describe a clear disconnection between polarized partisan elites and relatively unpolarized mass public (Lee, 2009; Lee, 2011). Yet, what is interesting is that this ideologically unpolarized mass public expresses polarized issue stances and support for candidates on various occasions (Kim, 2015b; Lee, 2011). The Korean electorate is malleable in its support for a political party. During the 17th Presidential election, a panel data ($N = 455$) showed that 28 percent of the Korean electorate changed their political allegiance during the campaign trail (Chung, 2011). What would drive political moderates (or Independents) to move toward one direction or the other? According to Kim (2015a), Korean Independents (1) are younger and more educated than partisans, (2) tend to believe their social status is relatively high, (3) come from more diverse regions across the nation, and most importantly, (4) show significantly different ideological orientations, policy preferences, and political attitudes from partisans. Kim (2015) noted Korean Independents are "issue public" who have certain political preferences but not able to find political parties to support. How do these Korean Independents respond to politically biased news stories? If there were any effect of news exposure, what are the mechanisms by which these effects are produced? These questions will significantly advance the current understating of how the media transfers elite polarization to the Korean mass public.

References

Aalberg, T., Stromback, J., & de Vreese, C. H. (2012). The framing of politics as strategy and game: A review of concepts, operationalizations and key findings. *Journalism*, 13(2): 162–178. doi:10.1177/1464884911427799

Abramowitz, A. I. (2010). *The Disappearing Center: Engaged Citizens, Polarization, and American Democracy*. New Haven: Yale University Press.

Arceneaux, K., & Johnson, M. (2014). *Changing Minds or Changing Channels?: Partisan News in an Age of Choice*. Chicago: University of Chicago Press.

Arceneaux, K., Johnson, M., & Cryderman, J. (2013). Communication, persuasion, and the conditioning value of selective exposure: Like minds may unite and divide but they mostly tune out. *Political Communication*, 30(2): 213–231. doi:10.1080/10584609.2012.737424

Auh, T.-S., & Park, S.-H. (2005). Hostile media perception in Korea: Message or messenger? *Korean Journal of Journalism & Communication Studies*, 49(2): 135–166.

Bennett, W. L., & Iyengar, S. (2008). A new era of minimal effects? The changing foundations of political communication. *Journal of Communication*, 58(4): 707–731. doi:10.1111/j.1460-2466.2008.00410.x

Cadinu, M., & Galdi, S. (2012). Gender differences in implicit gender self-categorization lead to stronger gender self-stereotyping by women than by men. *European Journal of Social Psychology*, 42(5): 546–551. doi:10.1002/ejsp.1881

Cappella, J. N., & Jamieson, K. H. (1997). *Spiral of Cynicism: The Press and the Public Good*. New York, NY: Oxford University Press.

Cho, E.-H., & Cho, S.-K. (2013). Diversity of media use and deliberative level: Focusing on moderating effect of selective exposure. *Journal of Communication Science*, 13(2): 370–396.

Choi, H.-J. (2010). A Study on the diversity of Korean newspapers: Analyzing the tendencies of covering three major issues. *Korean Journal of Journalism & Communication Studies*, 54(3): 399–426.

Choi, J. (2015). The effects of cross-cutting exposure in online social network sites on political participation: Focusing on the cross-cutting observation, cross-cutting involvement, and strength of partisanship. *Korean Journal of Journalism & Communication Studies*, 59(5): 152–177.

_____ (2016). The effects of SNS use on political participation: Focusing on the moderated mediation effects of politically-relevant social capital and motivations. *Korean Journal of Journalism & Communication Studies*, 60(5): 123–144.

Choi, J., Park, H. S., & Chang, J. J. (2011). Hostile media perception, involvement types, and advocacy behaviors. *Journalism & Mass Communication Quarterly*, 88(1): 23–39. doi:10.1177/107769901108800102

Choi, K.-J. (2003). A consideration of the conflicting relationship between government and media in Korea: Focused on media political actions of the participatory government.

Journal of Communication Science, 3(3): 95–132.

Choi, M. J., Kim, S. H., Kim, W. K., Park, D. M., Oh, S. W., & Choi, I. Do. (2016). *White Paper: 2016 Internet Press*. Seoul.

Choi, Y. (2016). How do we deal with nuclear energy issues?: A comparative analysis between press releases and newspaper articles. *Korean Journal of Journalism & Communication Studies*, 60(1): 229–262.

Choi, Y. J. (2014). Partisan schism in public broadcast newsroom: The paradox of democracy and political subordination. *Communication Theories*, 10(4): 476–510.

Choi, Y. J., & Lee, J. H. (2012). Cross-cutting exposure on the Internet discussion forums and its influence on political tolerance: A Mediation analysis of opinion modification and opinion polarization. *Korean Journal of Journalism & Communication Studies*, 56(2): 301–330.

Chung, H.-M. (2011). Influence of media and interpersonal communication on attitude change. *Korean Political Science Review*, 45(5): 243–272.

Coe, K., Tewksbury, D., Bond, B. J., Drogos, K. L., Porter, R. W., Yahn, A., & Zhang, Y. (2008). Hostile news: Partisan use and perceptions of cable news programming. *Journal of Communication*, 58(2): 201–219. doi:10.1111/j.1460-2466.2008.00381.x

Cohen, G. L. (2003). Party over policy: The dominating impact of group influence on political beliefs. *Journal of Personality and Social Psychology*, 85(5): 808–822. doi:10.1037/0022-3514.85.5.808

de Vreese, C. H. (2012). New Avenues for Framing Research. *American Behavioral Scientist*, 56(3): 365–375. doi:10.1177/0002764211426331

Dekavalla, M. (2016). Issue and game frames in the news: Frame-building factors in television coverage of the 2014 Scottish independence referendum. *Journalism: Theory, Practice & Criticism*, 146488491667423. doi:10.1177/1464884916674231

Druckman, J. N., & Bolsen, T. (2011). Framing, motivated reasoning, and opinions about emergent technologies. *Journal of Communication*, 61(4): 659–688. doi:10.1111/j.1460-2466.2011.01562.x

Druckman, J. N., Peterson, E., & Slothuus, R. (2013). How elite partisan polarization affects public opinion formation. *American Political Science Review*, 107(1): 57–79. doi:10.1017/S0003055412000500

Dunaway, J., & Lawrence, R. G. (2015). What predicts the game frame? Media ownership, electoral context, and campaign news. *Political Communication*, 32(1): 43–60. doi:10.1080/10584609.2014.880975

Fiorina, M., & Abrams, S. J. (2008). Political polarization in the American public. *Annual Review of Political Science*, 11: 563–588. doi:10.1146/annurev.polisci.11.053106.153836

Gaertner, L., Iuzzini, J., Witt, M. G., & Oriña, M. M. (2006). Us without them: Evidence for an intragroup origin of positive in-group regard. *Journal of Personality and Social Psychology*, 90(3): 426–439. doi:10.1037/0022-3514.90.3.426

Gentzkow, M., & Shapiro, J. M. (2011). Ideological segregation online and offline. *The*

Quarterly Journal of Economics, 126(4): 1799–1839. doi:10.1093/qje/qjr044

Hahn, K. S., Park, J.-Y., Lee, D.-J., & Lee, H.-L. (2013). A test of representativeness and polarization in twitter followership: A cross-national assessment of legislators' twitter followers in the U.S. and South Korea. *Journal of Cybercommunication Academic Society*, 30(1): 295–336.

Han, J., & Federico, C. M. (2017). Conflict-framed news, self-categorization, and partisan polarization. *Mass Communication and Society*, 20(4): 455–480. doi:10.1080/15205436. 2017.1292530

____. (in press). The polarizing effect of news framing: Comparing the mediating roles of motivated reasoning, self-stereotyping and intergroup animus. Accepted for publication in the *Journal of Communication*.

Han, J., & Wackman, D. B. (2017). Partisan self-stereotyping: Testing the salience hypothesis in a prediction of political polarization. *International Journal of Communication*, 11: 603–625.

Hart, P. S., & Nisbet, E. C. (2011). Boomerang effects in science communication: How motivated reasoning and identity cues amplify opinion polarization about climate mitigation policies. *Communication Research*, 39(6): 701–723. doi:10.1177/0093650211 416646

Hogg, M. A. (2003). Social identity. In M. R. Leary & J. P. Tangney (eds.). *Handbook of Self and Identity* (pp. 279–462). Guilford Press.

Hogg, M. A., & Turner, J. C. (1987). Intergroup behaviour, self-stereotyping and the salience of social categories. *British Journal of Social Psychology*, 26(4): 325–340. doi:10.1111/j. 2044-8309.1987.tb00795.x

Hollander, B. A. (2008). Tuning out or tuning elsewhere? Partisanship, polarization, and media migration from 1998 to 2006. *Journalism & Mass Communication Quarterly*, 85(1): 23–40.

Hong, J., & Son, Y. J. (2017). Korean media partisanship in the report on THAAD rumor: Network and frame analysis. *Korean Journal of Communication & Information*, 84: 152–188.

Hwang, C. S. (2007). A Study which how private opinion of conflicting issue and an attitude of individual newspaper effect perceived the bias of news and perceptions of public opinion. *Korean Journal of Journalism & Communication Studies*, 51(3): 308–327.

Hwang, W. S. (2013). Ideological polarization on Twitter from the perspectives of selective exposure. *Korean Journal of Journalism & Communication Studies*, 57(2): 58–79.

Iyengar, S., & Hahn, K. S. (2009). Red media, blue media: Evidence of ideological selectivity in media use. *Journal of Communication*, 59(1): 19–39. doi:10.1111/j.1460-2466.2008.01402.x

Iyengar, S., Sood, G., & Lelkes, Y. (2012). Affect, not ideology: A social identity perspective on polarization. *Public Opinion Quarterly*, 76(3): 405–431. doi:10.1093/poq/nfs 038

Jang, Y. J., & Lee, E.-J. (2010a). Effects of reading, writing, and opinion diversity in online discussion. *Korean Journal of Journalism & Communication Studies*, 54(2): 277–298.

_____ (2010b). How does message quality and opinion extremity moderate the effects of exposure to disagreement in online discussion? *Korean Journal of Journalism & Communication Studies*, 54(6): 422–443.

Jhee, B. K., Shin, D. C., & Eom, K. H. (2013). Exposure to conservative media and issue priority. *Journal of Contemporaty Politics*, 6(2): 127–155.

Jones, D. A. (2002). The polarizing effect of new media messages. *International Journal of Public Opinion Research*, 14(2): 158–174.

Kahan, D. M. (2013). Ideology, motivated reasoning, and cognitive reflection. *Judgment & Decision Making*, 8(4): 407–424.

Kang, J.-W., & Kim, S.-J. (2012). A study on the effect of comments posted under internet news articles: In consideration of the degree of involvement in issues and whether or not opinions are in accord. *Korean Journal of Journalism & Communication Studies*, 56(2): 143–166.

Kang, M. G. (2014). *Politicla Polarization after Democritizatio Movement and Its Remedies*. Seoul: National Assembly Research Service.

Kang, T. W., Ha, S. Y., Kim, J. H., & Kwan, H. (2014, January 8). Public goes to the center while partisan elites go to extreme: Politics aggravate social conflict. Joongang Il bo, A4. Seoul. Retrieved from http://news.joins.com/article/13584261

Kim, B., & Son, Y. (2015). The polarization effect of the Internet: Evidence from the Internet and TV users groups. *Information Society & Media*, 16(2): 17–45.

Kim, D. Y. (2015). Media manners and frames on the north korea nuclear test: Comparing with conservative, progressive and local newspaper. *Journal of Communication Science*, 15(1): 48–87.

Kim, E.-M., & Rhee, J. W. (2006). Rethinking "reading" online: The effects of online communication. *Korean Journal of Journalism & Communication Studies*, 50(4): 65–94.

Kim, E.-M., & Sun, Y.-H. (2006). The effect of replies in Internet news on the audience. *Korean Journal of Journalism & Communication Studies*, 50(4): 33–64.

Kim, H. (2016). The effect of hostile media perception on behavioral intention: The roles of political identity salience, emotions, and issue involvement. *Korean Journal of Journalism & Communication Studies*, 60(3): 66–90.

Kim, K., Lee, S. S., & Kim, S. J. (2016). Partisan audiences' hostile media perception and news media literacy: A theoretical amalgam of self-categorization and elaboration likelihood. *Communication Theories*, 12(3): 4–48.

Kim, S.-Y. (2015a). Ideology, policy preference, and political attitudes of independents in the 18th Korean presidential election. *Journal of International Area Studies*, 19(3), 149–171.

_____ (2015b). Polarization, partisan bias, and democracy: Evidence from the 2012 Korean Presidential Election panel data. *Journal of Democracy and Human Rights*, 15(3), 459–491.

Kim, S., & Park, S. G. (2010). How political meanings are generated in the economic crisis news: A case study of the broadcast news coverage during the 2008 financial crisis in South Korea. *Korean Journal of Journalism & Communication Studies*, 54(5): 301–326.

Kim, Y. (2011). Propaganda, conservatives, and the media: Analyzing the "Lost 10 Years" as propaganda strategies. *Korean Journal of Communication & Information*, 53: 100–120.

Kim, Y.-J., & Ha, S. (2014). Hostile media perception toward television news and the possibility of alternative use of Internet news. *Journalism & Communication*, 18(2): 57–87.

Kim, Y., Ham, S., & Kim, Y. (2017). Media discourse analyses on the Sewol Ferry incident: The methodological integration of the critical discourse analysis and the semantic Nnetwork analysis using newspaper big data. *Korean Journal of Communication & Information*, 83: 7–38.

Korea Press Foundation. (2016). *State of the News Media 2016*. Seoul. Retrieved from http://www.kpf.or.kr/site/kpf/mediasta/selectReceiverCodingList.do?cbIdx=249

Korean Center for Social Conflict Resolution & Hankook Research. (2017). *2017 Koreans' perception on social conflicts*. Seoul. Retrieved from http://kadr.or.kr/sub06/newsView.kadr?no=95&cpage=1

Kunda, Z. (1990). The case for motivated reasoning. *Psychological Bulletin*, 108(3): 480–498.

Kuppens, T., & Yzerbyt, V. Y. (2012). Group-based emotions: The impact of social identity on appraisals, emotions, and behaviors. *Basic and Applied Social Psychology*, 34(1): 20–33. doi:10.1080/01973533.2011.637474

Kuppens, T., Yzerbyt, V. Y., Dandache, S., Fischer, A. H., & van der Schalk, J. (2013). Social identity salience shapes group-based emotions through group-based appraisals. *Cognition & Emotion*, 27(8): 1359–1377. doi:10.1080/02699931.2013.785387

Layman, G. C., Carsey, T. M., Green, J. C., Herrera, R., & Cooperma, R. (2010). Activists and conflict extension in American party politics. *American Political Science Review*, 104(2): 324–346. doi:10.1017/S000305541000016X

Lee, E.-J. (2008). The economic crisis of the newspaper industry in Korea: Its causes and the structural problems. *Communication Theories*, 4(2): 73–111.

_____ (2011). Perceived bias or biased perception? Effects of others' comments, perceived opinion climate, and issue involvement on perceived news slant. *Korean Journal of Journalism & Communication Studies*, 55(3): 179–198.

Lee, E.-J., & Jang, Y. J. (2009). Effects of others' comments on internet news sites on perceptions of reality: Perceived public opinion, presumed media influence, and self-opinion. *Korean Journal of Journalism & Communication Studies*, 53(4): 50–71.

Lee, J. (2008). Korean journalism and social conflict. *Communication Theories*, 4(2): 48–72.

Lee, J. H. (2015). The effect of news audience's biased media perception on their evaluation of the media's fairness: A comparative analysis among congenial, neutral, and hostile media. *Korean Journal of Journalism & Communication Studies*, 59(1): 7–36.

Lee, J., & Lee, S.-K. (2016). The crisis of democracy and sensational partisan journalism: Focusing on political talk shows by Channel A and TV Chosun. *Korean Journal of Communication & Information*, 77: 9–35.

Lee, N.-Y. (2009). Changing ideological orientations and ideological voting of Korean voters. *Peace Studies*, 17(2): 42–72.

Lee, N. Y. (2017). Media use, the acquisition of misinformation, and political participation. *Korean Journal of Broadcasting and Telecommunication Studies*, 31(6): 118–151.

Lee, N. Y., & Cho, Y. (2017). Partisan knowledge learning or partisan interpretations: The influence of partisan media usage on attitude polarization toward partisan issues. *Korean Journal of Journalism & Communication Studies*, 61(5): 204–240.

Lee, S. (2011). The political polarization and the partisan sorting in Korean politics. *Journal of Democracy and Human Rights*, 11(3): 109–138.

_____ (2014). Party, media, and issue preferences: Media choice and political attitude in the 2014 Seoul mayoral election. *21st centry Political Science Review*, 24(3): 217–245.

_____ (2015). Media's mediating effects in the Korean election. *Korean Political Science Review*, 49(5): 287–313.

Leeper, T. J., & Slothuus, R. (2014). Political parties, motivated reasoning, and public opinion formation. *Political Psychology*, 35(S1): 129–156. doi:10.1111/pops.12164

Levendusky, M. (2009). *The Partisan Sort: How Liberals Became Democrats and Conservatives Became Republicans*. University of Chicago Press.

_____ (2013). Why do partisan media polarize viewers? *American Journal of Political Science*, 57(3): 611–623. doi:10.1111/ajps.12008

Levendusky, M., & Malhotra, N. (2016). (Mis)perceptions of partisan polarization in the American public. *Public Opinion Quarterly*, 80(S1): 378–391. doi:10.1093/poq/nfv045

Lodge, M., & Taber, C. S. (2013). *The Rationalizing Voter*. New York: Cambridge University Press.

Mackie, D. M. (1986). Social identification effects in group polarization. *Journal of Personality and Social Psychology*, 50(4): 720–728. doi:10.1037/0022-3514.50.4.720

Mackie, D. M., & Cooper, J. (1984). Attitude polarization: Effects of group membership. *Journal of Personality and Social Psychology*, 46(3): 575–585. doi:10.1037/0022-3514.46.3.575

Mackie, D. M., Devos, T., & Smith, E. R. (2000). Intergroup emotions: Explaining offensive action tendencies in an intergroup context. *Journal of Personality and Social Psychology*, 79(4): 602–616.

Min, H., & Lee, W.-T. (2015). Voter's ideological orientation and media use. *Korean Party Studies Review*, 14(1): 157–176.

Min, Y. (2016). Citizens' selective news use in an election: The causes and political consequences of partisan selectivity and news selectivity. *Korean Journal of Journalism & Communication Studies*, 60(2): 7–34.

Nam, S. W. (2009). The crisis of Korean press and responsibilities of professional journalists. *Kwanhun Journal*, 113: 89–111.

Nicholson, S. P. (2012). Polarizing Cues. *American Journal of Political Science*, 56(1): 52–66. doi:10.1111/j.1540-5907.2011.00541.x

Oakes, P. (2002). Psychological groups and political psychology: A response to Huddy's

"Critical Examination of Social Identity Theory." *Political Psychology*, 23(4): 809–824. doi:10.1111/0162-895X.00308

Oakes, P., Turner, J. C., & Haslam, S. A. (1991). Perceiving people as group members: The role of fit in the salience of social categorizations. *British Journal of Social Psychology*, 30(2): 125–144. doi:10.1111/j.2044-8309.1991.tb00930.x

Onorato, R. S., & Turner, J. C. (2004). Fluidity in the self-concept: The shift from personal to social identity. *European Journal of Social Psychology*, 34(3): 257–278. doi:10.1002/ejsp.195

Otten, S., & Mummendey, A. (2000). Valence-dependent probability of ingroup favouritism between minimal groups: An integrative view on the positive-negative Asymmetry in social discrimination. In D. Capozza & R. Brown (eds.). *Social Identity Processes: Trends in Theory and Research* (pp. 34–48). London: SAGE Publications. doi:10.4135/9781446218617.n3

Park, J. H. (2016). Estimation of media slants in South Korean news agencies using news reports on the Sewol Ferry disaster. *Korean Political Science Review*, 50(1): 239–269.

Park, S.-G., & Chang, K.-S. (2000). Political transition and changes in the state-media relationship in Korea. *Korean Journal of Broadcasting and Telecommunication Studies*, 14(3): 81–113.

Park, S. W. (2014). Why does the political polarization continue in SNS?: Focusing on the subject of the communication, the reliability of the information in the types of SNS and the trust of other people. *Social Science Research Review*, 30(1): 235–252.

Park, Y., & Kim, K. (2016). Journalism as a ritual: For a new understanding of partisan journalism in Korea TT -. *Korean Journal of Journalism & Communication Studies*, 60(1): 202–228.

Patterson, T. E. (1993). *Out of Order: An Incisive and Boldly Original Critique of the News Media's Domination of America's Political Process*. New York: Knopf.

Pew Research Center. (2013). *Partisan Polarization, in Congress and Among Public, Is Greater Than Ever*. Retrieved from http://www.pewresearch.org/fact-tank/2013/07/17/partisan-polarization-in-congress-and-among-public-is-greater-than-ever/

_____ (2014, March). State of the News Media 2014 Key Indicators in Media & News. Retrieved from http://www.journalism.org/2014/03/26/state-of-the-news-media-2014-key-indicators-in-media-and-news/

Price, V. (1989). Social identification and public opinion: Effects of communicating group conflict. *Public Opinion Quarterly*, 53(2): 197–224. doi:10.1086/269503

Prior, M. (2013). Media and political polarization. *Annual Review of Political Science*, 16: 101–127. doi:10.1146/annurev-polisci-100711-135242

Redlawsk, D. P. (2002). Hot cognition or cool consideration? Testing the effects of motivated reasoning on political decision making. *The Journal of Politics*, 64(4): 1021–1044. Retrieved from http://journals.cambridge.org/abstract_S0022381600001614

Reid, S. A. (2012). A Self-Categorization Explanation for the Hostile Media Effect. *Journal of Communication*, 62(3): 381–399. doi:10.1111/j.1460-2466.2012.01647.x

Rhee, J. W., & Choi, Y.-J. (2005). Causes of the crisis in Korean newspapers: Functional displacement in media use, provision of lower value, and trust crisis. *Korean Journal of Journalism & Communication Studies*, 49(5): 5–35.

Roh, J.-K., & Min, Y. (2012). Effects of politically motivated selective exposure on attitude polarization: A study of non-political online community users. *Korean Journal of Journalism & Communication Studies*, 56(2): 226–248.

Roh, S., Choi, J., & Min, Y. (2017). Correlates of fake news effects: Identifying facilitating and constraining factors on fake news exposure and acceptance in the 2017 Korean presidential election TT—Correlates of fake news effects: Identifying facilitating and constraining factors on. *Journal of Cybercommunication Academic Society*, 34(4): 99–149.

Rojas, H. (2010). "Corrective" actions in the public sphere: How perceptions of media and media effects shape political behaviors. *International Journal of Public Opinion Research*, 22(3): 343–363. doi:10.1093/ijpor/edq018

Schmuck, D., Heiss, R., Matthes, J., Engesser, S., & Esser, F. (2017). Antecedents of strategic game framing in political news coverage. *Journalism: Theory, Practice & Criticism*, 18(8): 937–955. doi:10.1177/1464884916648098

Shin, D. H., & Lee, J. H. (2014). Does survey response on the use of Internet news sites reflect actual use of the sites?: An exploration of selective exposure and in-group bias. *Korean Journal of Broadcasting and Telecommunication Studies*, 28(4): 157–197.

Slothuus, R., & de Vreese, C. H. (2010). Political parties, motivated reasoning, and issue framing effects. *The Journal of Politics*, 72(3): 630–645. doi:10.1017/S00223816100000 6X

Son, Y.-J. (2004). The effects of media use on conservative and progressive opinion. *Korean Journal of Journalism & Communication Studies*, 48(2): 240–266.

Song, H.-J., Shin, S.-M., & Park, S.-G. (2006). Reading dissonant opinions on the Internet and its effects on argument repertoire and tolerance. *Korean Journal of Journalism & Communication Studies*, 50(5): 160–183.

Song, I. (2014). Biased media perception based on media partisanship and audience's political disposition: In case of newspaper editorials. *Communication Theories*, 10(3): 222–257.

Stroud, N. J. (2008). Media use and political predispositions: Revisiting the concept of selective exposure. *Political Behavior*, 30(3): 341–366. doi:10.1007/s11109-007-9050-9

_____ (2010). Polarization and partisan selective exposure. *Journal of Communication*, 60(3): 556–576. doi:10.1111/j.1460-2466.2010.01497.x

Tajfel, H., & Turner, J. C. (1979). An integrative theory of intergroup conflict. In W. G. Austin & S. Worchel (eds.). *The Social Psychology of Intergroup Relations* (Vol. 33, pp. 33–47). Montery, CA: Brooks-Cole.

Tajfel, H., & Turner, J. C. (1986/2004). The social identity theory of intergroup behavior. In J. T. Jost & J. Sidanius (eds.). *Political Psychology: Key Readings* (pp. 276–293). New York, NY: Psychology Press.

Turner, J. C., Hogg, M. A., Oakes, P., Reicher, S. D., & Wetherell, M. S. (1987).

Rediscovering the Social Group: A Self-Categorization Theory. Oxford, UK: B. Blackwell.

Turner, J. C., Oakes, P., Haslam, S. A., & McGarty, C. (1994). Self and collective: Cognition and social context. *Personality and Social Psychology Bulletin*, 20(5): 454–463. doi:10.1177/0146167294205002

Vallone, R. P., Ross, L., & Lepper, M. R. (1985). The hostile media phenomenon: Biased perception and perceptions of media bias in coverage of the Beirut massacre. *Journal of Personality and Social Psychology*, 49(3): 577–585.

van Klingeren, M., Boomgaarden, H. G., & de Vreese, C. H. (2017). Will conflict tear us apart? The effects of conflict and valenced media messages on polarizing attitudes toward EU immigration and border control. *Public Opinion Quarterly*, 81(2): 543–563. doi:10.1093/poq/nfw051

Yang, H. S. (2008). The effects of the opinion and quality of user postings on Internet news readers' attitude toward the news issue. *Korean Journal of Journalism & Communication Studies*, 52(2): 254–281.

Yoon, I. J. (2015). Current Situations and Changes of Koreans' Perceptions of Social Conflict. *Korean Society*, 16(1): 3–36.

digital
KOREA

Mediated Presence of Korean Religion in the Digital Era

Intersecting with Issues and Discussions of 'Media and Religion' Scholarship

4

SEUNG SOO KIM

Chulalongkorn University

INTRODUCTION

The title of guest editors' introduction to the special issue of *The Journal of Korean Religions*, "Religion and Media: No Longer a Blindspot in Korean Academia" (Park, Cho, & Han, 2017), reflects the fact that 'media and religion' has not received a proper scholarly interest in Korea. Along with Jin-Kyu Park's pioneering studies on the intersection between televised media and religion in Korea (2006, 2007, 2008a), the special issue would be counted as one of the rare moments where a good deal of scholarly discussion is given to the intersection between media and religion.[1] Given the

---

1 Jin-Kyu Park's research on media and religion in Korea includes the production and reception of religious symbolism in Korean TV serial (2006, 2007, 2008a), Korean journalistic discourse on religion (2008b, 2015), the theoretical and methodological approach to the intersection between media, religion, and culture (2009), and healing culture (2016). He had been the sole researcher who consistently examined the interaction between the two until a few scholars' works on media and religion began to be published in 2016. Recent research on media and religion in Korea covers the perception of Korean Christianity as a cultural villain (Hong, 2016), the circulation of social imaginaries on Korean Protestantism and Buddhism through digital media (Kim, 2016), the history of Korean religious broadcasting (Lee, 2017), the significance of newspapers to the early

general lack of research on relations of media and religion in general, it is no surprise that the intersection between digital media and religion is significantly under-researched in Korea. It is quite symptomatic that, even in the special issue, relatively little attention was given to the intersection between digital media and contemporary religion (e.g. Kim, 2017) while the historicity of relations between media institutions and religion in Korea acquired a well-deserved scholarly attention (e.g. Lee, 2017; Noh, 2017; Cho, 2017).

Facing such lack of scholarly interest in digital media and religion, I take this book chapter as an invaluable opportunity to introduce not only my research on digital media and Korean religion but also key issues and theoretical discussions in the scholarship of media and religion. Thus, this chapter surveys some of the issues and discussions which have been crucial to the scholarship of media and religion and my works as well. They include media supersaturation (Couldry, 2012), the thesis of secularization in media studies (Morgan, 2013; Stolow, 2005), mediatisation and mediation of religion (Hjavard, 2008, 2009; Lundby, 2009; Meyer, 2011, 2014; Morgan, 2013), and the third spaces which digital religion affords and generates (Hoover & Echchaibi, Forthcoming). This chapter interweaves these various issues and theoretical discussions with the research on the mediated presence of Korean religion in digital space (Kim, 2016, 2017), while oscillating between the two. To provide a detailed, critical survey of the scholarship of media and religion is much necessary but beyond the focus of this chapter. I hope it could provide a touchstone for public and scholarly discussions on digital media and religion in the Korean context.

KOREAN BUDDHISM IN THE DIGITAL ERA

As the internet, smartphone, and social networking sites have come to be increasingly penetrated in everyday practices of meaning-making, social

Korean Protestant community (Noh, 2017), the construction of religion in Korean news media (Cho, 2017), and the branding of Templestay in digital space (Kim, 2017).

interaction, community building, and information and emotion sharing, people in the late-modern societies have encountered a condition of what Couldry (2012) calls "the supersaturation of society by media" where social life is excessively "filled with media contents at every level" (Couldry, 2012: 5). According to statistics, Koreans are obviously living in one of the most media-saturated societies in the world.[2] In such condition, media are increasingly inevitable and definitive of everyday experience in both the private and the public spheres. As Hoover (2016) puts, "we do not see media as one marketplace among many or one shelf among many in a broad inventory of symbolic resources. Instead, for both structural reasons and reasons of practice, the media are the context, they are the inventory" (Hoover, 2016: 24). It is increasingly the case that religions come to exist in clear, defined, and popular forms as religions try to survive an ever-expanding cultural marketplace of choice and practice, which is often called 'the media.' In other words, religions must 'brand' themselves to exist, sustain, and reproduce their public presence in the media (Hoover, 2016; Hoover & Kim, Forthcoming).

In the Korean context, Buddhism, the allegedly traditional and monastic Korean religion, has been arguably better at 'branding' its public presence in the media, especially in digital media, than Protestantism (Kim, 2016). *Authenticity, Brand Culture, and Templestay in the Digital Era* (Kim, 2017) explores how the branding of Templestay in digital media newly shape the mediated presence of Korean Buddhism, nothing Korean Buddhism's

---

2 The internet penetration rate of South Korea in 2010 was 81.1%. The 2014 rate was stated at 84.8% (www.internetworldstats.com, last accessed on August 20th, 2014). The 2017 rate was 92.7% (http://www.internetworldstats.com/asia/kr.htm, accessed on February 23rd, 2018). Meanwhile, South Korea was having the cheapest and fastest broadband in the World around the time of 2012 (http://www.nytimes.com/2011/02/22/technology/22iht-broadband22.html?_r=1&, last accessed on February 23rd, 2018). In addition, in 2005 already, 96.8% of Korean mobile phones had internet access (Ahonen & O'Reilly, 2007: 242). According to the OECD historical mobile broadband penetration rates, the wireless mobile broadband penetration rate of South Korea in 2017 is 111.09% (https://data.oecd.org/broadband/wireless-mobile-broadband-subscriptions.htm, last accessed on February 23rd, 2018).

interwoven relationships with the state's heritage policies, spiritual tourism, contemporary brand culture, and digital media. Templestay is the cultural experience program accommodating foreign and domestic tourists to Buddhist Temples in Korea. The Cultural Corps of Korean Buddhism, in charge of the promotion and operation of Templestay, has actively used a variety of digital media including YouTube,[3] Facebook,[4] Twitter,[5] Pinterest,[6] E-Magazine,[7] and official websites[8] to attract not only domestic but also foreign visitors and it has achieved a great success.[9] The research focuses on the ways in which digital media come to be appropriated as a site for Korean Buddhism to newly imagine, contextualize, legitimize, and brand its public presence in the allegedly Westernized, urbanized, and globalized social world.

The active appropriation of digital media by The Cultural Corps of Korean Buddhism is significantly interwoven with neo-liberal branding practices. Banet Weiser (2012) finds that in neo-liberal brand culture authenticity itself becomes brand as allegedly authentic spaces, such as religion, creativity, and the self, are increasingly visualized, recognized and experienced in and through the logic of brand. She argues that neoliberal brand culture is characterized by the building of the affective, intimate, and authentic relationship between brand and consumers and the relationship is

---

3   http://www.youtube.com/user/TEMPLESTAYALL?feature=watch,   accessed   February 27th, 2018.

4   https://www.facebook.com/templestay, accessed February 27th, 2018.

5   https://twitter.com/templestaykorea, accessed February 27th, 2018.

6   http://www.pinterest.com/templestaykorea/templestay-korea,   accessed   February   27th, 2018.

7   http://www.templestay.com/common/media/magazine.asp?c_idx=15,   accessed   February 27th, 2018.

8   http://www.templestay.com; http://eng.templestay.com/index.asp, accessed February 27th, 2018.

9   "The number of participants in the program in 2004 was 52,549, though the number of foreign participants was only 6,617. But in 2009, the total number of participants was 140,893, with foreign participants now 19,399 (CCKB 2010, 4). In 2014, the number of participants in Templestay reached 193,388, with the number of foreigners at 25,560" (Kim, 2017: 122).

increasingly afforded, sustained, and expanded by digital media including social networking sites. The in-depth interview with Templestay's PR and R&D managers, who are in charge of the branding of Templestay, interestingly manifests how their view on new digital media aligns with Banet-Weiser's remark on neoliberal brand culture and the significance of digital media to it (Kim, 2017: 124):

> Both the PR and R&D managers point out that television broadcasts in particular have a massive impact on the public. However, it is new digital social media that the managers imagine as the venue by which the most "important" and "successful" branding has been and should be done. New digital media is preferred because it affords so-called viral marketing and enables the sharing of authentic personal narratives on Templestay by past and future visitors. The R&D manager stated that "the actual photographs taken by Templestay participants and their personal narratives on their experience [of Templestay] are most important [in branding]." The PR manager also asserted that "people come to want to join Templestay because of the texts or photographs which other Templestay participants posted sharing their [Templestay] experience with the participants [through digital media]." In this way, the branding of Templestay in digital space comes "to draw people to our side." But this takes time. New digital media "is about sustainability rather than about immediate effect," the PR manager adds. She continues:
>
> Through [digital social] media we inform [potential participants in Templestay] that we do this and that thing. Then, this becomes like a communication between individuals. In Facebook, though we don't know each other, we come to know things like, "oh, this person came here" and "my post reached those people."

The quotation from the PR manager illuminates that she finds digital media enabling and affording an intimate and personal relationship not only between Templestay and its online visitors but also among them. Then, what are the imaginaries and imageries of Korean Buddhism which the brand builders try to embed in consumers' everyday "memories, emotions, personal narratives, and expectations" (Banet-Weiser, 2012:8)? Among many digital materials of the branding of Templestay, the first 90 seconds of the English-language Templestay promotion video on its YouTube channel, would best exemplify the public presence of Korean Buddhism that it wants to legitimize and brand.[10] The scenes could be broken down into as follows (Kim, 2017):

> The video's opening shows four contrasting images of hands, feet, thinking, and eating in a modern metropolis versus a Buddhist temple. While one's hands in the city touch a computer keyboard and smartphone screen, a person in the temple calmly touches a flower and prays while caressing Buddhist beads. After showing these scenes, the video presents to silence the English words, "Give peace to your busy hands." And while the feet of commuters hurriedly climb the concrete stairs of a subway station, a visitor slowly ascends the stone steps of a Buddhist temple. Again, after these scenes, the video presents to silence the English words, "Allow your feet to relax." While a worker in a skyscraper elevator keeps ascending, a visitor modestly bows in Buddhist ritual. In silence then appear the English words, "Humble your mind and lower yourself." Lastly, while people leave food like large cuts of meat on their plates, visitors in Templestay carefully savor the seemingly simple and wholesome Korean Buddhist fare. Then in English appears, "Emptiness and peace of mind," again in silence (Kim, 2017: 132).

Through the scenes, the late-modern urban life is portrayed as artificial, distracted, and avaricious, in contrast with the Templestay experience depicted as nature-friendly, monastic, humble, simple, and peaceful. The late-modern metropolis comes to be represented as inauthentic and un-

10 https://www.youtube.com/watch?v=oKYMj4QGooQ, accessed on February 27th, 2018.

spiritual space that corrupts, distracts, and exhausts city dwellers, rather than simply neutral, physical location. On the contrary, Buddhist temples, as an embodiment of Korean Buddhism, are "imagined and narrativized, not as mere tourist attraction, but as authentic spiritual space that can transform one's habits of mind and body and, more essentially, one's self" (Kim, 2017: 135).

In the early modern era, Korean Buddhism was considered as the religion of hermits, children, and women who were rarely thought of as public and political existence (Lee, 2000). Buddhism was not able to make its public and political voice in late Joseon until Japanese Buddhism helped Buddhist monks to enter the capital of Joseon on 1895 (Lee, 2000; Kim, 2012). While the imageries of childlikeness, femininity, and seclusion would likely have been an obstacle for Korean Buddhism to acquiring public and political recognition in early modern Korea, now they help Korean Buddhism be associated with imageries and ideas of innocence, purity, monasticism, and authenticity—in fact all of things that are often imagined as lost in, or corrupted by, the process of urbanization and technology-driven modernization (Kim, 2017). As shown in the scenes introduced above, Korean Buddhism finds its *raison d'être* to be a spiritual antidote to the ill and fatigue of technology, modernization, and urbanization while erasing its histories closely interwoven with them.

For instance, for Korean Buddhism, it was not separable between its modernization and Japanese Buddhism given that modernized Buddhism was seen and experienced primarily in and through the mediation of Japanese Buddhism in early modern Korea (Cho, 2006, 2010). But as the Chogye Order has held hegemony since the 1950s, efforts to modernize Buddhism in the Japanese colonial era, including the destruction of celibacy, the allowance of meat-eating, and the acceptance of and learning from Japanese Buddhism, have been increasingly stigmatized as the pro-Japanese acts to corrupt the authenticity and tradition of Korean Buddhism. The Chogye Order has been quite successful in constructing its ahistorical self-identity: the authentic inheritor and guardian of Korean Buddhist tradition free from the mixture with, and the contamination by, the forces of the outer world including Japanese colonialism and modernization. The contemporary branding of Templestay in digital spaces should be understood in light of Korean Buddhism's ongoing historical project of reproducing its ahistorical identity where it is imagined as distanced from any contact with and contamination by modernization, technology, urbanization, and domestic and international politics. Further, contrary to its branded imagery of monasticism distancing from modern technology, the digital branding of Templestay paradoxically demonstrates the dilemma of Korean Buddhism whose project of legitimizing and sustaining its public presence, cannot be successfully done without media in the media-saturated Korea (Kim, 2017).

THE RETURN (OR PERSISTENCE) OF RELIGION IN THE LATE-MODERN SOCIAL WORLD

The inevitable intersection between Korean Buddhism and the digital is not exceptional in any sense. Researchers interested in the intersection between media and religion increasingly find that media have been not only a primary space where the presence of religion is manifested, branded, legitimized, and contested, but also a central form shaping the beliefs, rituals, and communities that we count as religious and/or spiritual today (Hjavard, 2011; Hoover, 2006; Hoover & Echchaibi, Forthcoming; Meyer, 2006, 2014; Stolow, 2005). Such view of media as enabling and shaping the contemporary presence of religion, however, seems quite contradictory to a widely-accepted secularist discourse about modern media which are considered to damage religious authorities' control over their laity and further serve for the decline of religion as mediator and facilitator of modernization. Ironically, Christian authorities have been ones of those who most strongly hold and express such secularist view on media.[11] In Korean society as well,

11 The long history of Christian critique of, and fear over, modern media, could be exemplified by some cases from the efforts of the Catholic Church in the 16th century to prohibit the circulation of printed material to the North American evangelists' rituals of publicly burning Harry Potter books in the 21st century (Stolow, 2005: 120–121).

Protestant churches have been very influential as 'censoring power.' Films such as *The Last Temptation of Jesus Christ* and *The Da Vinci Code* encountered campaigns against their release while being accused of blasphemy. TV programs revealing the corruption of prominent pastors have been put into the danger of not being broadcast due to the severe protests of believers following the pastors.

It is noteworthy that, for both religious authorities worrying such secularist role of modern media and others celebrating it, there persists the widely-accepted idea of secularization that modernity inevitably leads to the decline of religion (Stolow, 2005). Media studies has not been exceptional in taking the secularization thesis for granted. Morgan (2013) offers a rough, but largely undeniable, remark on the troubled and contested presence of religion in media studies:

> For its part, media studies has happily presumed that religion expired somewhere between the French Revolution and Marxism's dismissal of religion as the opiate of the masses, a largely inert pacifier that was no match for more interesting distractions such as entertainment media. Secularization was supposed to mean that the nasty incursion of religion into public life would be no more and that the secular state, safely insulated from ecclesiastical control, would arise. Disestablishment happened, to be sure, but religion did not go away (Morgan, 2013: 349).[12]

Hoover and Kim (Forthcoming) argue that Protestantism in North America has held an ambivalent attitude toward media. On one hand, based on the secularist view on media, it has constantly aspired to regulate the process and practices of modern mediation between the religious and public culture. On the other hand, however, it has also aspired to be a public voice of morality in and through mass media.

12 The general lack of interest in religion in media and cultural studies in Korea could not be irrelevant to the legacy of British cultural studies which have been significantly indebted to Marxism and much less interested in critical engagement with religion, compared to its remarkable studies on race, gender, sexuality, and social class. See also Stolow (2005) and Morgan (2013) regarding the lack of interest in religion in British Cultural Studies and Marxism.

Contrary to the received idea that modernity would cause its decline, religion has been increasingly prominent and influential in contemporary political discourses and imaginaries in the U.S., Europe, India, and the Middle East, to name a few.[13] When it comes to Korean society, modernity has rarely brought the decline of religion, if not in a normative sense. Contrary to the contemporary popular discourse on Korean Protestantism, which is imagined as an annoying but powerful agent impeding the development and modernization of Korean society, Protestantism has been significantly interwoven with the imaginaries and discourses on civilization, modernization, and progress until the recent history of Korea (Jang, 1999; Kim, 2016; Lee, 2000).[14] Meanwhile, Korean Buddhism which has been consid-

---

13 It turns out that the relationship between modernity and religion is more complicated than what the secularization thesis suggests. The prominence of fundamentalist religious movements in contemporary politics is partially indebted to late-modern conditions. Both contemporary forms of right-wing nationalism and fundamentalist religions find each other useful and encouraging in mass-mobilizing people who desperately seek for certainty and security in their disgust at increasing fluidity, uncertainty, and disintegration — all of things that are considerably generated by the intensification and acceleration of global move and circulation of capital, labor forces, refugees, tourists, images, texts, objects, and technologies, to name a few, in the late-modern era (Appadurai, 1996; Harvey, 2005; Rosa, 2003).

14 Not a few intellectuals and political elites in early modern Korea embraced Protestantism in their expectation that Protestantism would help modernize and strengthen Korea enough to protect it from surrounding powers such as China, Russia and Japan (Jang, 1999). New education and medical services brought into Korea by Western missionaries were experienced as the advance of the Western modern civilization (Lee, 2000). Since the establishment of South Korean government right after the Korean War, Protestant churches have demonstrated a strong connection with political elites of the United States which has been often imagined as a strong force and model for Westernization and modernization in Korean society (Baek, 2014). Meanwhile, during the period of the so-called 'compressed modernization' from the 1960s to the 1980s, the incredible growth of Korean Protestantism as a popular urban religion accompanied with the intensification of urbanization, industrialization, and westernization of Korean society (Yang, 2012). Further, the Protestant discourse circulated in the early modern era to legitimate the superiority of Protestantism over other religions, have undeniably affected how modernity is imagined and discussed in Korean society. The separation between religion and politics was suggested by early Western missionaries in Korea as the principle of the

ered as the religion of a long-preserved tradition and monasticism, has come to emerge as one of the latest spiritual antidotes to the ill and fatigue of individuals living in the increasingly competitive late-modern society (Kim, 2016). The rise of monk Haemin as media celebrity in 'healing culture' (Park, 2016) and the branding of Templestay in digital space (Kim, 2017), to name a few, exemplify the increasingly prominent and alternative presence of Korean Buddhism in the contemporary media landscape of late-modern Korea.

MEDIATIZATION AND MEDITATION OF RELIGION

The increasing intersections between media and religion and their significance to the contemporary social world, have generated vibrant and growing scholarly discussions on 'mediatization' and 'mediation' of religion. In Hjavard's original formulation, mediatization theory argues that social structures and institutions come to embrace and employ the forms which media produces as the social world comes to be super-saturated by media and thus "society to an increasing degree is submitted to, and becomes dependent on, the media and their logic" (Hjavard, 2009: 160).[15] In such perspective, Hjavard's work (2008) on the mediatization of religion explores in what ways the decline of religious participation in Denmark could be understood in the context of media supersaturation. It illustrates examples where media become a language which molds "religious imaginations in accordance with the genres of popular culture" and seem to replace "the social functions of institutionalized religion, providing moral and spiritual guidance and a sense of community" (Hjavard, 2008: 9). Important critiques

modern state and as the significant criteria to judge what the authentic modern religion is (Lee, 2000, Jang, 1999). Further, while pushing almost every traditional Korean religion into the category of superstition/shamanism or that of philosophy, Protestantism contributed to the dissemination of what could be called the modern dichotomy between religion and philosophy, religion and superstition, in Korean society (Lee, 2000).

15 However, his position regarding mediatization was revised on 2011. See Hjavard (2011).

were provided to the theory of the mediatization of religion.[16] For instance, Hoover and Echchaibi (Forthcoming) argue that it is preoccupied mainly with traditional, institutionalized, large, and public religions while over-looking what happens in the digital spaces where "social actors are using the digital precisely to work against the dominant, unitary views of religion" (Hoover & Echchaibi, Forthcoming: 29). Lundby (2009) points out that Hjavard tends to mask and mystify the media logic by not examining how its process takes places in and by concrete social practices producing and con-suming the media forms for spiritual and religious work. Couldry (2012) ar-gues that it is media-centric and lacks specificity considering the single media logic cannot "explain the range of general effects to which mediatiza-tion theorists claim to point" (Couldry, 2012: 136).

Contrary to the seemingly presentist view of 'mediatization' which high-lights that religion comes to be increasingly subject to, and shaped by, the logic of 'contemporary media,' the 'mediation' view highlights "continuities in the ways in which religions have always been mediated, and sees more modern means of mediation, such as in the digital realm, as evolutions, rather than disruptions" (Hoover & Echchaibi, Forthcoming: 27)[17] According to Birgit Meyer (2006, 2014), postulating and drawing a boundary between human being and the transcendental, religions provide, circulate, discipline, and pass on practices and technologies of mediation through which the distance between the two can be bridged and make it possible to sense and experience the transcendental. Similarly, Orsi (2005) remarks that "religion is the practice of making the invisible visible . . . to render them visible and tangible, present to the senses in the circumstances of everyday life" (Orsi, 2005: 147). In the 'mediation' view, media is defined, not "in the narrow, familiar sense of modern mass media, but in the broad sense of transmitters across gaps and limits" (Meyer, 2014: 216). What makes spiritual imaginaries about sacred and divine being visible, tangible, and graspable, is all kinds of

16 For the mediatization debate, see Couldry (2012: 135–137).

17 For proponents of the 'mediation' view, 'mediatization' theory is seen somewhat ahis-torical, presentist, and technologically-deterministic. Regarding the 'mediation' view, see Meyer (2006, 2011, 2014), Morgan (2007), Orsi (2005), and Stolow (2005, 2010).

media that simultaneously mediate and materialize them.[18] Media encompass a variety of religious dress, texts, imageries, rituals, practices, and spaces —what Meyer (2006, 2014) calls 'sensational forms' which tend to structure sensory experiences of the transcendental.

In this view, the idea of 'media' and 'religion' acting upon each other as fixed and separate domains, is hardly held. Rather, they are understood as coming together and having fundamental commonalities than largely assumed. Importantly, both media and religion accompany practices and technologies of mediation of 'imaginaries'.[19] "The media work in the same turf as religion, in registers of imagination, and can, through mediations of imagination and experience, interpose themselves into spaces and modes that were once more the monopoly of 'the religious (Hoover & Echchaibi, Forthcoming: 31).'" In the media-suffused Korean society, digital media enable and afford practices of mediation and circulation of imaginaries almost everywhere, anytime. Digital media in the Korean context could be arguably explored as mediated and networked social space where imaginaries and experiences regarding religions are significantly constructed, mediated, circulated, received, and contested. For instance, examining the mainstream liberal online media's coverage of Korean Protestantism and its reception in the 2012 Lady Gaga controversy and the 2015 knife attack on the US ambassador,[20] a case study in my dissertation finds that digital media come to be a crucial site for the construction, mediation, and circulation of imaginaries about Korean Protestantism, whose presence in contemporary Korea is imagined and experienced as anachronistic, irrational, dangerous, and further threatening the complete modernization and civilization of Korea

18 Regarding the simultaneity of mediation and materialization, see Appadurai (2015).
19 Anderson (1991) and Appadurai (1996), for instance, highlight the increasing significance of media technology in mediating and circulating imagination which is essential to the construction and reproduction of the modern social world.
20 In the 2012 Lady Gaga controversy, Korean Protestants made several public protests and prayer meetings against the Lady Gaga concert and homosexuality. In the 2015 knife attack on the US ambassador to South Korea, a Protestant group publicly performed shamanistic rituals to worship the U.S. and console its ambassador. Both incidents caused a controversy over the public presence of Korean Religion in contemporary Korean society.

(Kim, 2016).[21]

THIRD SPACES OF DIGITAL RELIGION

Roughly speaking, religion has not gone away. Participation in institutional-ized religion may have been decreased in media-saturated societies including South Korea.[22] Instead, new practices, aesthetics, locales, and presences of religion have emerged in the digital era (see Campbell, 2013; Helland, 2016; Hoover & Kim, 2016 for the discussions of digital religion). The decline of institutionalized religion might be the flip side of the rise in 'personal au-tonomy' in matters of religious belief and practice. Individuals increasingly imagine their spirituality/religiosity as an ongoing project of achievement for their personal needs, rather than merely as belonging to religious institution (Hammond, 1992; Roof 1999). In such context, "individuals use the tech-nical capacities of the digital to imagine" new and hybrid identities, prac-tices, and communities of religion "beyond the existing binaries of the physi-cal versus the virtual, the real versus the proximal religious experience" (Hoover & Echchaibi, Forthcoming: 25).

Although not all online materials and networks could be identified 'third spaces,' in certain contexts and moments, the digital arguably hosts hybrid performance and practice through which individuals "self-consciously nego-tiate a place for themselves over against" and beyond existing binaries preva-lent in their social world (Hoover & Echchaibi, Forthcoming: 24). Other

21 Meanwhile, the other case study illuminates that a variety of digital media used by Templestay constructs, mediates, and circulates particular imaginaries about Korean Bud-dhism, whose presence is imagined as monastic, innocent, authentic, and even curing the ill and fatigue of urbanization and modernization (Kim, 2016).

22 "The population with religion decreased from 52.9 percent in 2005 to 43.9 percent in 2015. The population without religion increased from 47.1 percent in 2005 to 56.1 percent in 2015 (Results of the 2015 Population and Housing Census, last accessed on February 25th, 2018 at http://kostat.go.kr/portal/eng/pressReleases/8/7/index.board?b mode=read&bSeq=&aSeq=361147&pageNo=1&rowNum=10&navCount=10&currPg= &sTarget=title&sTxt=)"

binaries transgressed or hybridized by digital practices include: authority and autonomy, commodities and authenticity, individual and community, and tradition and secularism. Hoover and Echchaibi illuminate that in the generative encounters between the binary poles hosted by digital practices, there emerge the 'ambivalence,' 'in-between-ness,' and 'third-ness' of religious ideas, practices, and communities that are newly contested, imagined, negotiated, reconstructed, thought of, and expressed beyond the binaries. Digital media facilitate and afford 'third spaces' for individuals or even institutions looking for more autonomy and creativity in their religious or spiritual work.[23] Often against established religion and existing binaries, they find opportunities and possibilities for their work in digital spaces. They act 'as-if' they were already communities of a shared idea, sentiment, and experience and their new ways of imagining and thinking about 'the religious' were already accepted and shared by their imagined communities as truth. Hoover and Echchaibi conceptualize such digital site of cultural production of the newly imagined 'religious,' characterized by 'in-between-ness' and 'as-if-ness,' as the third space of digital religion.

The branding of Templestay in digital space arguably generates the in-between-ness and ambivalence of mediated presence of Korean Buddhism. My research finds that Templestay is "not entirely a sacred heritage, nor is it a secular accommodation; not fully monasticism, nor tourism; not absolutely an authentic spirituality, nor a commercial product; and not completely a local, Korean tradition, nor a global popular culture" (Kim, 2017: 139).[24]

---

23 This metaphor of the 'third spaces' of digital religion heavily draws on Homi Bhabha's term of 'Third Space' in postcolonial theory, space typified by negotiation, ambivalence, and hybrid and in-between subjectivity, in which individuals self-consciously "negotiate, subvert and reread the signs and symbols of colonial power" in the imbalanced encounter "between a hegemonic colonial authority and a subordinate indigenous culture" (Hoover & Echchaibi, Forthcoming: 23).

24 "To regard Templestay as a mere commercialization or marketing of Korean Buddhism, does not correctly capture the current presence of Korean Buddhism. As Banet-Weiser puts it, "branding is different from commercialization or marketing" given that it is "deeply, profoundly cultural" and thus ambivalent (2012, 14). In-between-ness and ambivalence are not only the characteristics of digitally mediated religion but that of the

Rather than falling into one of the binaries between the two poles, the digital branding of Templestay hosts a constant oscillation, encounter, and negotiation between them. It is argued that the public presence of Korean Buddhism shaped by the branding of Templestay is ambivalent, in-between, or hybrid given that its mediated presence constantly oscillates between the local and the global, monasticism and tourism, the traditional and the modern, authenticity and commodity, and the sacred and the secular. Although Templestay is an institution, it acts 'as-if' it is an individual in digital space. In Facebook, for instance, it 'shares,' 'likes,' and 'comments' on other Facebook users' posts. in the same way that individuals newly imagine and work on their spirituality/religiosity in digital space, Templestay appropriates digital media to transform the earlier location, form, and face of the institutionalized religion of Korean Buddhism. That is, the branding of Templestay in digital space can be understood as a reflexive project of Korean Buddhism to newly imagine and legitimize its self-identity, spirituality, and public presence in the digital media landscape of late-modern Korea.

CONCLUDING REMARKS

From the 'mediation' view that highlights practices of mediation in exploring 'media and religion,' it is seen that the contemporary penetration and dissemination of digital media in everyday practices shapes an emergent social condition in which 'the religious' comes to be newly defined, imagined, and experienced. Increasing social practices of mediation and circulation of imaginaries related to 'the religious' leave the definitions, boundaries, forms, and faces of both 'the digital' and 'the religious' open to change in the contemporary social world. This change is never homogeneous across the world and history. It is contingent to the social and historical context in which media and religion have been imagined, thought of, practiced, and experienced (see, for example, Hoover and Kim, Forthcoming; Kim, 2017). I hope

branding of neo-liberal times (Kim, 2017: 139)"

this chapter could be useful to those who want to explore and research digital media and religion in the broader context of social and historical change. A variety of theoretical and empirical issues regarding digital media and religion in the Korean context wait for public and scholarly interests. It would be very pleasing if this chapter could contribute to their initiation.

References

Ahonen, T. & O'Reilly, J. (2007). *Digital Korea: Convergence of Broadband Internet, 3G Cell Phones, Multiplayer Gaming, Digital TV, Virtual Reality, Electronic Cash, Telematics, Robotics, E-Government and the Intelligent Ho.* London: Futuretext.

Anderson, B. (1991). *Imagined Communities: Reflections on the Origin and Spread of Nationalism* (Rev. and extended Ed.). London: Verso.

Appadurai, A. (1996). *Modernity at Large: Cultural Dimensions of Globalization.* Minneapolis, Minn.: University of Minnesota Press.

____ (2015). Mediants, materiality, normativity. *Public Culture,* 27(2): 221–237.

Baek, J. H. (2014). *Taet'ongyŏngkwa chongkyo (President and religion: How religion became power).* Seoul: Inmulkwa Sasang.

Banet-Weiser, S. (2012). *Authentic TM: Politics and Ambivalence in a Brand Culture.* New York: New York University Press.

Campbell, H. (ed.) (2013). *Digital Religion: Understanding Religious Practice in New Media Worlds.* London: Routledge.

Cho, K. H. (2017). "Religion in the press: The construction of religion in the Korean news media." *Journal of Korean Religions,* 8(2): 61–89.

Cho, S. T. (2006). Kŭntae pulkyohakkwa hankuk pulkyo (Modern Buddhist Scholarship and modern Korean Buddhism). *Minchok Munhwa Yŏnkuwŏn (Research Institute of Korean Studies),* 45: 77–109.

____ (2010). Kŭntae hankuk pulkyosa kisulŭi munche: Minchokchuŭichŏk yŏksa kisule kwanhan pip'an (Reconsidering the nationalist historiography of Modern Korean Buddhism). *Minchok Munhwa Yŏnkuwŏn (Research Institute of Korean Studies),* 53: 581–620.

Couldry, Nick (2012). *Media, Society, World: Social Theory and Digital Media Practice.* London: Polity.

Hammond, P. E. (1992). *Religion and Personal Autonomy: The Third Disestablishment in America.* Columbia: University of South Carolina Press.

Harvey, D. (2005). *A Brief History of Neoliberalism.* Oxford: Oxford University Press.

Helland C. (2016). Digital Religion. In D. Yamane (ed.). *Handbook of Religion and Society.* Cham: Springer.

Hjarvard, S. (2008). The mediatization of religion. A theory of the media as agents of religious change. *Northern Lights,* 6(1): 9–26. doi: 10.1386/nl.6.1.9/1

____ (2009). Soft individualism: Media and the changing social character. In K. Lundby (ed.). *Mediatization: Concept, Changes, Consequences.* (pp. 159–177). New York: Peter Lang.

____ (2011). The mediatisation of religion: Theorising religion, media and social change. *Culture and Religion,* 12(2): 119–135. https://doi.org/10.1080/14755610.2011.579719

Hong. S. M. (2016). Uncomfortable proximity: Perception of Christianity as a cultural villain in South Korea. *International Journal of Communication,* 10: 4532–4549.

Hoover, S. (2006). *Religion in the Media Age.* London & New York: Routledge.

_____ (2013). Evolving religion in the digital media. In Knut Lundby (ed.). *Religion across Media: From Early Antiquity to Late Modernity*. London: Peter Lang.

_____ (2016). Religious authority in the media age. In S. Hoover (ed.). *The Media and Religious Authority*. University Park: The Pennsylvania State University Press.

Hoover, S. & Kim, S.S. (2016). Media. In D. Yamane (ed.). *Handbook of Religion and Society*. Cham: Springer.

_____ (Forthcoming). A Protestant vision of digital media. In S. Hoover & N. Echchaibi (eds.). *The Third Spaces of Digital Religion*. In press (The Pennsylvania State University Press).

Hoover, S. & Echchabi, N. (Forthcoming). Theory and context: The third space of digital religion. In S. Hoover & N. Echchaibi (eds.). *The Third Spaces of Digital Religion*. In press (The Pennsylvania State University Press).

Jang, S. M. (1999). Kŭntaemunmyŏng ilanŭn ilŭmŭi kaesinkyo (The Protestantism called modern civilization). *Yŏksa Pip'yŏng (History Critique)*, 46: 255–268.

Kim, S. S. (2016). *Imagining Religion and Modernity in Post-Colonial Korea: Neo-Liberal Brand Culture and Digital Space*. Doctoral Dissertation. University of Colorado-Boulder.

_____ (2017). Authenticity, brand culture, and Templestay in the digital era: The ambivalence and in-betweenness of Korean Buddhism. *Journal of Korean Religions*, 8(2): 117–146. Project MUSE, doi:10.1353/jkr.2017.0015

Kim, Y. T. (2012). Hankuk kŭntaepulkyoŭi chongkyochŏk mosaekkwa chwachŏl (The religious seeking of Korean modern Buddhism and its frustration). *The 31st Conference of the Research Institute of Won-Buddhist Thought* (pp. 69–80). Retrieved from http://www.dbpia.co.kr/Journal/ArticleDetail/NODE02395500

Korean Chogye Order, Cultural Corps of Korean Buddhism (CCKB) (Taehan pulgyo chogyejong han'guk pulgyo munhwa saŏpdan) (2010). Tempŭl sŭtei 2010 saŏp kyehoek [Templestay 2010 business plan]. Seoul: Taehan pulgyo chogyejong.

Lee, J. G. (2000). Kŭntae hankuk kaesinkyowa pulkyoŭi sanghoinsik (Mutual perception between Protestantism and Buddhism in Modern Korea). *Chongkyo Munhwa Yŏnku (Religious Cultural Studies)*, 2: 145–164.

Lee, S. M. (2017). A history of religious broadcasting in Korea from a religious politics standpoint: Focusing on the period of a Protestant broadcasting monopoly. *Journal of Korean Religions*, 8(2): 11–31. Project MUSE, doi:10.1353/jkr.2017.0011

Lundby, K. (ed.) (2009). *Mediatization: Concept, Changes, Consequences*. New York: Peter Lang.

Meyer, B. (2006). *Religious Sensations. Why Media, Aesthetics and Power Matter in the Study of Contemporary Religion*. Inaugural Lecture (6th, October), VU University, Amsterdam.

_____ (2011). Mediation and immediacy: sensational forms, semiotic ideologies and the question of the medium, *Social Anthropology*, 19(1): 23–39.

_____ (2014). Around Birgit Meyer's "Mediation and the genesis of presence: Toward a material approach to religion". *Religion and Society: Advances in Research*, 5: 205–254.

Morgan, D. (2007). *The Lure of Images: A History of Religion and Visual Media in America*. London: Routledge.

____ (2013). Religion and media: A critical review of recent developments. *Critical Research on Religion*, 1(3): 347–356.

Noh, M. J. (2017). The role of newspapers in the early Korean Protestant community: An analysis of the Korean Christian Advocate and the Christian News. *Journal of Korean Religions*, 8(2): 33–60. Project MUSE, doi:10.1353/jkr.2017.0012

Orsi, R. (2005). *Between Heaven and Earth: The Religious Worlds People Make and the Scholars Who Study Them*. Princeton, NJ: Princeton University Press.

Park, J. K. (2006). Media, religion, and culture in contemporary Korea: Production and reception of religious symbolism in a daily TV Serial. Doctoral dissertation. University of Colorado, Boulder.

Park, J. K. (2007). Reading patterns for media text with religious symbolism: Diverse Responses to TV Serial "Wang-kkot Seon-nyeo-nim." *Korean Journal of Journalism & Communication Studies*, 51(6): 381–410. Retrieved from http://www.dbpia. co.kr/ Article/NODE00955836

____ (2008a). Planning and production of a television serial with religious symbolism and mysticism: A case study of code-breaking series. *Korean Journal of Journalism & Communication Studies*, 52(4): 324–352. Retrieved from http://www.dbpia.co.kr/ Article/NODE01060225

____ (2008b). Justifying the media's production of religious discourse: A case study of TV documentary <God's Way, Man's Way>. *Korean Journal of Broadcasting and Tele-communication Studies*, 22(6): 110–148. Retrieved from http://www.dbpia.co.kr/ Article/NODE01094604

____ (2009). Media, religion, and culture: A new approach to the study on the intersections between media and religion. *Korean Journal of Journalism & Communication Studies*, 53(6): 309–329. Retrieved from http://www.dbpia.co.kr/Article/NODE01312905

____ (2015). Mediated religion and social change: Discursive construction of Pope Francis's visit to Korea by Journalism. *Korean Journal of Communication & Information*, 70: 221–245. Retrieved from http://www.dbpia.co.kr/Article/NODE06268272

____ (2016). 'Healed to imagine': healing discourse in Korean popular culture and its politics. *Culture and Religion*, 17(4): 375–391.

Park, J. K., Cho, K., & Han, S. (2017). Religion and media: No longer a blindspot in Korean academia. *Journal of Korean Religions*, 8(2): 5–10. Project MUSE, doi:10.1353/ jkr.2017.0010

Roof, W. C. (1999). *Spiritual Marketplace: Baby Boomers and the Remaking of American Religion*. Princeton: Princeton University Press.

Rosa, H. (2003). Social acceleration: Ethical and political consequences of a de-synchronized high speed Society. *Constellations*, 10(1): 3–33.

Stolow, J. (2005). Religion and/as media. *Theory, Culture & Society*, 22(4): 119–145.

____ (2010). *Orthodox by Design: Judaism, Print Politics, and the Art Scroll Revolution*. University of California Press.

Yang, H. S. (2012). *Dasi, Protestant (Again, Protestant)*. Seoull: Bock Itnuen Saram.

digital
KOREA

Pharmaceutical Marketing in the Digital Era

How It Adapts to Digital Environments

5

HEEWON IM

The Nielsen Company Korea

Because their products are closely tied to physicians' practices, pharmaceutical companies' marketing activities are geared toward physicians and focus on providing medical information through various methods (Yi, 2017). The medical information usually consists of the most up-to-date clinical study outcomes that show the positive aspects of their pharmaceutical products. To deliver this commercially edited medication information in a more effective way, pharmaceutical companies are also carefully investigating the channel to deliver their commercial message.

Digital sources have become an integral part of physicians' practices to receive medical information updates. Although previous studies on physicians' medical information seeking demonstrate that physicians still trust traditional sources more than digital sources, they are now using both traditional (e.g., guidelines, textbooks, and drug references) and digital sources (e.g., online drug information, mobile medical guidelines, and online medical news) for updating their medical information, both during or after their practices (Haug, 1997).

To adapt to physicians' transition from traditional sources to digital sources for their medical information updates, pharmaceutical companies are now devising and implementing several digital marketing activities to reach their target consumers, such as webinar/web symposiums and e-detailing. Although previous studies on physicians' perception of commercial sources have demonstrated physicians' relatively low trust on commercial sources and their reluctance to accept that commercial sources influence them (Spiller & Wymer, 2001), physicians in real practice have used commercial sources as a beneficial and convenient source of medical information (Spiller & Wymer, 2011). Particularly, clinic physicians, due to their different work environment than physicians who work at general hospitals, are now relying more and more on commercial digital medical information sources for medical information updates.

This essay examines how "going digital" has been applied in pharmaceutical marketing communication and how it changes information seeking behavior for healthcare products' most important consumers in Korea: clinic physicians, such as internists, family doctors, and general practitioners (IM/FM/GP). More specifically, the essay will consider how pharmaceutical companies have been adapting to the digital environment and developing marketing communication strategies to reach physicians, as well as how these pharmaceutical companies' digital marketing strategies (e.g., web symposiums, e-detailing) could help physicians update their medical information in the digital era. This study will specifically focus on pharmaceutical marketing toward clinic physicians in Korea.

CHARACTERISTICS OF PHARMACEUTICAL MARKETING

To understand the unique aspects of pharmaceutical marketing, it is necessary to understand the healthcare system itself. As with any other product, the pharmaceutical product exchange involves more than two parties. However, unlike general consumer goods, where the end-user/consumer, manufacturer, and distributers exchange goods and services directly with each other, pharmaceutical products, particularly prescription medication or devices, require a physician's prescription, involving an intermediary when making purchase decisions and when paying the manufacturer (Belsey,

2007). Four stakeholders, the physician (prescriber), pharmacist, payer, and patients, are involved in this unique product exchange process. The four stakeholders take different forms depending on each country's healthcare system; however, they typically play the following roles:

Patients

The patient is the end-user of pharmaceutical products. They request a healthcare service from physicians, and the physicians examine and diagnose their condition and decide whether to prescribe pharmaceutical products.

Prescriber

Prescribers are usually healthcare providers who have a license to diagnose and treat patients when they visit for healthcare services, and they are allowed to prescribe healthcare products, including pharmaceutical products, to patients if needed. The definition of a prescriber is different depending on the healthcare system. For example, in the U.S. or New Zealand, not only physicians but also registered nurses or nurse practitioners and some other healthcare providers can write a prescription for some pharmaceutical products, such as the flu vaccine (Fong, Buckley, & Cashin, 2015). In Korea, only physicians and dentists can write prescriptions (Article 18, Medical Service Act, No.14438, 2016). By identifying and reviewing the patient record, prescribers decide whether to prescribe certain pharmaceutical products to their patients, who are the end-users. Once prescribed, the prescription is sent to a pharmacist for dispensing.

Pharmacist

A pharmacist is a pharmaceutical product dispenser in the healthcare system. Pharmacists dispense medication based on the prescription received from the doctor. By reviewing the physician's prescription and the patient's history through their computer or other intermediary hub, they refill the request from patients (Minnesota Department of Health [MDH], 2015).

Payer

Unlike fast-moving consumer goods (FMCG), such as diapers, whose purchase decision is made by one consumer, the end-user, purchasing pharmaceutical products involves a unique stakeholder known as the payer. Payers are organizations purchasing healthcare services for patients who are subscribed to their services (MDH, 2015). In many healthcare systems, payers are health insurance institutions, which can be either private or government institutions. Korea is one of the countries that has a national, universal healthcare system (Song, 2009). Payers typically store subscribed patients' health insurance information (including prescription benefits and history) and send it to physicians through a certain system when requested.

CHARACTERISTICS OF PHARMACEUTICAL MARKETING IN KOREA

Because of the differences in healthcare systems and regulations in each country, the roles and relationships among the aforementioned four stakeholders varies. Therefore, pharmaceutical marketing must adapt to each country's unique healthcare system. Although some private health insurance companies still exist, Korea has a universal healthcare system: all Korean citizens are required to be insured to National Health Insurance Services in various forms through their workplace, regional government offices, or as a dependent of another Korean citizen (Song, 2009). Unlike healthcare systems where several private health insurance companies play a major role as payers, Korean patients basically rely on one universal health insurance reimbursement policy, which may limit their choice and involvement with their healthcare-related decision-making process. This also means that *the payer* is basically a government officer. From the pharmaceutical companies' perspective, payers in Korea cannot be the target of their direct promotion.

Since 2000, the Korean healthcare system has separated drug prescriptions and the dispensing system. Before the separation, both doctors and pharmacists prescribed and dispensed drugs to patients. After several discussions with the relevant associations, drug prescribing and dispensing was finally separated in 2000. Now, only doctors and dentists can write a prescription, and only pharmacists can dispense the drug (Article 18, Medical Service Act, No. 14438, 2016). Therefore, in terms of the prescription medication exchange process, physicians play a more active role in the choice of medication. Of course, in the universal healthcare system, physicians', particularly clinic physicians', prescriptions are dependent on the reimbursement guidelines and regulations from the National Health Insurance Review and Assessment Service (HIRA); however, physicians still play the major role in choosing the prescribed medication. This study will focus on pharmaceutical marketing toward physicians.

PHARMACEUTICAL MARKETING: TRANSITION TO DIGITAL FORMATS

Since their products' features, such as efficacy and safety, must be based on clinical trial outcomes, pharmaceutical companies' marketing activities target the medically trained individuals who make purchase decisions for their practices; thus, pharmaceutical companies' marketing activities are geared toward physicians and focus on providing medical information through various marketing strategies (James, 2004, as cited in Belsey, 2007). The medical information usually consists of the most up-to-date clinical study outcomes that show the positive aspects of their pharmaceutical products.

Traditionally, pharmaceutical marketing, particularly prescription medication marketing, relies on detailing from sales representatives (through physical visits with the physician and meeting face-to-face; Belsey, 2007). However, some changes in this traditional approach have occurred with the move to digital sources, which have become an integral part of physicians' practices. Although previous studies on physicians' medical information seeking demonstrate that physicians still trust traditional sources more than digital sources, they are now using both traditional (e.g., guidelines, textbooks, and drug references) and digital sources (e.g., online drug information, mobile medical guidelines, and online medical news) for updating their medical information (Bellman, Havens, Bertolucci, & Streeter, 2005).

In Korea, the transition to digital marketing for physicians has quickened due to two strict regulations: the Improper Solicitation and Graft Act (Jang, 2017) and the K-Sunshine Act (Choi, 2017). The Improper Solicitation and Graft Act, also known as the Kim Young Ran Act, which regulates the limit of complementation to government officers when meeting or contacting them in regard of their roles or works (Improper Solicitation and Graft Act, No. 14183, 2016). Since most general hospitals are teaching hospitals at colleges, most general hospital physicians and some clinic physicians who work as instructors are bound to this Act, which in turn, limit pharmaceutical companies marketing to the physicians who bound to the Act. In addition, the K-Sunshine Act, which became effective in January 2018 (Lee, 2018), further regulates the pharmaceutical industry's marketing activities. Even before the K-Sunshine Act, pharmaceutical companies' direct rebates were impounded, for both the pharmaceutical companies and the physicians who received the improper rebates (Ministry of Health and Welfare [MOHW], 2018). In addition, there is a two-strike-out policy for improper rebates, and it was first applied in 2017 to Norvatis Korea, which had violated its rebate offer twice. As a result, Norvatis had to pay 5,6100,000,000 Korean won as a penalty, and some of the company's products were suspended from the NHI reimbursement list for a limited time (Choi, 2017). The K-Sunshine Act goes further and makes it mandatory for pharmaceutical companies to report any financial compensation sent to healthcare providers (Choi, 2017). The two Acts have strictly regulated face-to-face pharmaceutical marketing activities, accelerating pharmaceutical marketing's transition to digital (Jang, 2017).

To adapt to the physicians' transition from traditional sources to digital sources for their medical information updates and to the strictly regulated Korean pharmaceutical market, pharmaceutical companies are now devising and implementing several digital marketing activities to reach their target consumers. Some examples of these digital marketing activities include information web pages, webinar/web symposiums, e-detailing, and web portal services.

Online Information Services

Pharmaceutical companies are managing medical information web pages, where they provide the most up-to-date information regarding their products and the relevant diseases, including summarized versions of recent study results. Furthermore, some pharmaceutical companies provide a database of journal article abstracts (e.g., MSD Korea's MD faculty, Janssen Korea's JannsenPro) or even services that provide continuing medical education (CME).

Table 1. Examples of Online Information Services

MSD Manual (MSD Korea)	• MSD Korea's medical information websites, both for healthcare providers and patients

MDfaculty	• MSD Korea's web portal for medical information
	• Contents:
	  ◦ CME (online education)
	  ◦ Journal articles
	  ◦ Medical information about diseases

Merck Biopharma GM Academy+ (Merck Korea)	• Merck Korea's medical information web portal • Format: web and mobile • Content: ◦ Up-to-date medical information on diabetes, dyslipidemia, and cariology

MediDocLink /MediDoc Link M (Pfizer Korea)	• Pfizer Korea's medical information platform for Pfizer product-related disease information
	• MediDoc Link: web platform
	• MediDoc Link M: started in July 2017, mobile platform for smartphone and tablets
	• Contents:
	  ◦ Medication information on diseases
	  ◦ Webinars on diseases, including cardiovascular (CV) disease, central nervous system (CNS) disease, and chronic pain.

Pfizer Medical Information (Pfizer Korea)	• Pfizer Korea's web platform for up-to-date Pfizer product-related medical information

Janssen PRO (Janssen Korea)	• Janssen Korea's web portal
	• Contents:
	  ○ Janssen product information and relevant medical information
	  ○ Patient education materials
	  ○ Real-time online CME

Webinar/Web Symposium

Pharmaceutical companies provide webinar or web symposium services to physicians to update their medical information on various diseases and treatment patterns/trends. Typically, the lecturer of the webinar or web symposium is a national or international key opinion leader (KOL) in their respective medical field and share various up-to-date medical information and the clinical outcomes from recent studies. The webinar/web symposium can be either a simultaneous broadcast of an actual event or a recorded version of it.

Table 2. Examples of Webinars/Web Symposiums

GSK On-Air in Health.gsk (GSK Korea)	• local/international webinar from GSK
LINKsium (Pfizer Korea)	• Pfizer Korea's webinar platform • Contents: ○ local/international webinar on Pfizer product-related medical information
Live web seminar and video replay in LillyON (Lilly Korea)	• Live web seminar: online webinar • Video replay: webinar archive
Live symposium in HMP (Hanmi Pharmaceuticals)	• Live symposium: webinar on medical information

E-detailing

E-detailing is an online version of detailing services but mostly focuses on providing the most up-to-date medication information related to the companies' products or relevant disease areas. Typically, there is an e-detailing representative, and a detailing appointment is made before the service (e.g., Pfizer Korea's Pfizerlink and MSD Korea's MSD CallME); clinic physicians can choose the time that they are available for the service. When making the appointment, physicians can also choose the topic of the detailing services, such as specific disease areas and the most up-to-date reimbursement guidelines for prescription treatments. At the appointment time, the e-detailing representative directly calls the clinic physician and deliver information on the chosen topic for 5 to 10 minutes. During the detailing session, physicians also log in to the e-detailing service website and can see the e-detailing representative and the supporting materials, such as slides based on recent study results. Recently, some pharmaceutical companies have also conducted chat sessions for e-detailing services (e.g., GSK Korea's Medichat) so that physicians can interact with e-detailing representatives whenever they need medical information about the companies' products or the relevant diseases being treated.

Table 3. Examples of e-detailing

Medi-chat in Health.GSK (GSK Korea)	• Real-time chat/e-detailing for medical information

MSD CallME	• MSD Korea's e-detailing service
	• Contents:
	  ◦ Up-to-date medical information about MSD products and their related diseases
	  ◦ Patient education materials

PfizerLink (Pfizer Korea)	• Pfizer Korea's e-detailing service • Contents: ◦ Pfizer product-related medication/disease information that meets the needs of physicians
e-Academy in LillyON (Lilly Korea)	• e-Academy: e-detailing service

Web Portal/Multi-Channel Marketing (MCM) Platform

Recently, pharmaceutical companies have called the aforementioned digital activities multi-channel marketing (MCM) and have tried to provide this as a more comprehensive experience for physicians. One such approach is to design a web portal/MCM platform where physicians can experience diverse digital marketing activities in one place. For example, in 2017, GSK Korea started the *Health.GSK* service, which provides comprehensive medical information for physicians regarding GSK products and patient education materials for e-detailing services. Lilly Korea also manages the *LillyON* service, which provides webinar/web symposium services for e-detailing.

Table 4. Examples of web portals/MCM platforms

Health.GSK (GSK Korea)	• GSK Korea's web portal for Korean physicians • Started in November 2017 • Format: web and mobile • Contents: ◦ Information about GSK products and their relevant diseases, including pulmonology, HIV, urology, and Dermatology ◦ Patient education materials for physicians ◦ GSK On-Air: local/international webinar from GSK ◦ Medi-Chat: real-time chat/e-detailing for medical information
MSD CallME	• MSD Korea's e-detailing service • Contents: ◦ Up-to-date medical information about MSD products and their related diseases ◦ Patient education materials
Merck Biopharma GM Academy+ (Merck Korea)	• Merck Korea's medical information web portal • Format: web and mobile • Content: ◦ Up-to-date medical information on diabetes, dyslipidemia, and cariology
MediDocLink /MediDoc Link M (Pfizer Korea)	• Pfizer Korea's medical information platform for Pfizer product-related disease information • MediDoc Link: web platform • MediDoc Link M: started in July 2017, mobile platform for smartphone and tablets

	• Contents: ○ Medication information on diseases ○ Webinars on diseases, including cardiovascular (CV) disease, central nervous system (CNS) disease, and chronic pain.
LillyON (Lilly Korea)	• Lilly Korea's multi-channel marketing platform • Contents: ○ Live web seminar: online webinar ○ Video replay: webinar archive ○ Medical square: medical information and academic information ○ e-Academy: e-detailing service ○ Lilly Product: Lilly product information
Janssen PRO (Janssen Korea)	• Janssen Korea's web portal • Contents: ○ Janssen product information and relevant medical information ○ Patient education materials ○ Real-time online CME
HMP (Hanmi Pharmaceuticals)	• Hanmi's medical information web portal • Contents: ○ Live symposium: webinar on medical information ○ KIMS/MEDLINE/PubMed: information on medication, journal article/abstract ○ Knowledge Q&A: bulletin board for exchange medical information ○ Clinic/Hospital Management Solution: consulting management solution

Current Status of Pharmaceutical Digital Marekting

Korean digital marketing activities tend to be led by multinational (MNC) pharmaceutical companies, such as Pfizer Korea, MSD Korea, and GSK Korea. Basically, all companies have an MCM approach to digital marketing for physicians by implementing various activities, from webinars to e-detailing; however, how they implement each activity is different: some pharmaceutical companies already provide several services in separate platforms, while others tend to approach physicians with one MCM platform.

Pfizer Korea and MSD Korea present several services in separate platforms. For example, Pfizer Korea develops and provides separate services for online information (Pfizer Medical Information and MediDoc Link), webinars/web symposiums (LinkSIUM), and e-detailing (PfizerLINK). Even online information services are divided into a disease-focused information web page (MediDoc Link) and a product-focused information page (Pfizer Medical Information). With this approach, pharmaceutical companies try to provide more specialized services for each digital marketing activity. Typically, pharmaceutical companies take this approach to digital marketing in Korea. For instance, in 2013, Pfizer Korea's PfizerLink was the first e-detailing service launched in Korea (Song, 2015). Since these companies are the pioneers of digital marketing services in a market where the concept of digital marketing, such as e-detailing, had never existed, providing separately targeted services could be beneficial to familiarize physicians with such services.

The companies who provide digital services tend to take a web portal/MCM approach by providing one platform that provides multiple digital marketing services. GSK Korea, Lilly Korea, Janssen Korea, and Hanmi pharmaceuticals are examples of companies taking this approach. The companies typically manage one web page that enables physicians to explore multiple services provided by pharmaceutical companies. For example, at Heatlh.GSK, visitors can view the webinar of their choice (GSK On-Air), get GSK product information, and even chat with representatives for more medication information (MediChat).

NEXT STEP FOR DIGITAL MARKETING FOR RESEARCHERS: What Will Be the Actual Influence on Physicians' Practices and Overall Public Health Costs

Role of Digital Marketing Activities as Medical Information Source

Although CME run by medical associations exist for maintaining their board-certified status, previous studies on physicians' perception of commercial sources demonstrate physicians have less trust for commercial sources (Spiller & Wimer, 2001). However, commercial sources have been used as a beneficial and convenient source of medical information for physicians in real practice (e.g., Prosser & Walley, 2003).

Particularly, clinic physicians, due to their tight work schedules, need medical resources that are easily accessible at any time and place and that are formatted in a more comprehensive way so that the information can be applied immediately. Physicians are already updating their medical knowledge (63%) through the Internet because of its convenience (Bellman et al., 2005); however, a comparison of Bennett and colleagues' results from three surveys showed that physicians have been increasingly frustrated by the amount of online medical information that is available and find it difficult to search for specific information at the same time (Bennett et al., 2004, 2006). Since digital marketing services tend to provide information in a comprehensive way at a convenient time and place, it can serve as a CME or at least an RSS feed or quick reminder of up-to-date medical information for clinical physicians.

Furthermore, because physicians are already highly trained and have medical knowledge, they tend to think they can selectively acquire only the necessary and accurate information from even commercial sources, and they tend to show a positive perception on medication information from commercial sources, such as sales representatives (Fisher et al., 2009; Spiller & Wymer, 2011). Physicians' confidence in their ability to process medical knowledge, even from commercial sources, and their positive attitude toward information from pharmaceutical companies show the possibility that pharmaceutical digital marketing can serve as a medical information source and CME resource for them.

However, academic research on the potential role of pharmaceutical marketing on physicians' medical information seeking is scarce, particularly in Korea, and there have been no empirical studies in this area. There are some studies on more traditional pharmaceutical marketing activities, such as sales representatives (e.g., Cha, Ryu, & Lee, 2013; Jung, Ahn, & Yi, 2017; Yi, 2017). However, no specific empirical study has been conducted on digital pharmaceutical marketing's role in physicians' medical information seeking. Future research must focus on this area.

Impact of Digital Marketing on Physician's Prescription Pattern

Another research area that needs attention is the actual impact on digital pharmaceutical marketing on physicians' prescription patterns. Because the primary purpose of pharmaceutical marketing is it to increase physicians' prescriptions of promoted branded products, it is crucial to assess whether the hypothesized influence is observable in real practice. Some studies show a mixed relationship between pharmaceutical marketing on physicians' prescription behavior (for a literature review, see Squrling et al., 2010); however, more empirical studies on the relationship have not been conducted in the context of digital pharmaceutical marketing at the individual level. More empirical research need to be conducted to test the relationship between digital pharmaceutical marketing and physicians' prescription patterns.

NEXT STEP FOR DIGITAL MARKETING FOR MARKETERS: Which Contents Should Be Provided to Physicians and How Can Digital MCM Effectiveness Be Measured

Optimal Contents for Physicians

For pharmaceutical marketers to develop an effective marketing strategy, it is critical to learn what kind of information physicians need and how to deliver it. First, to learn about the physicians' needed information, it is necessary to know the underlying motivation of physicians' information seeking. Physicians have two basic information needs: (1) the need to learn about their patients' conditions and (2) the need to learn about treatment modalities, procedures, equipment, and medications (Case, 2008). Accordingly, physicians tend to seek medical information required for making medical decisions, such as diagnoses and prescriptions, for updated knowledge, and/or for conducting evidence-based practice.

Specifically, physicians want to learn more practical information that they can apply to solve their patients' issues. Casebeer et al. (2002) showed that the needs to learn about particular patients' problems and to update medical knowledge highly motivate physicians to seek information online. Similarly, Bennett and colleagues (2005) demonstrated that the primary motivation for seeking medical information online is a specific patient problem. The tendency is found more among general practitioners than specialists. One study from the U.S. shows that, compared to specialists, primary care physicians are more likely to go online to search for information applicable to their actual practice (Casebeer et al., 2002).

The study results from examining the online medical information seeking of physicians, particularly general practitioners such as clinic IM/FM/GP, suggest that online sources could be effective for delivering the most up-to-date clinical study results about diseases and their products; however, such sources also need to provide information about how to actually apply this knowledge to their actual practice. To meet this need, some pharmaceutical companies already provide patient education materials to support physicians' practices; however, also providing case studies of actual patient treatments from KOL or other physicians via e-detailing or webinars/web symposiums or interactive scenarios programmed into the CME could be useful in meeting the clinic IM/FM/GPs' needs.

Measuring MCM Effectiveness

As the ultimate goal of pharmaceutical marketing is maximizing revenue, it is critical to measure marketing activity effectiveness. Pharmaceutical companies have already devised various measures for traditional marketing activity, such as a sales representative's call effectiveness, visit frequency, and visit quality (detailing rate and detailed message recall from physicians), to investigate the actual contribution to the promoted product's prescription rate.

However, as digital marketing is incorporated into the traditional marketing activities, it is getting more challenging for the pharmaceutical marketers to measure the effectiveness not only of digital marketing activities but also MCM as a whole. As more and more pharmaceutical companies take the MCM approach for their pharmaceutical product marketing, the market research industry will also try to provide some answers for measuring its effectiveness. For example, one healthcare market research company, GfK, suggests that the effectiveness of MCM activities should be evaluated based on whether each channel meaningfully reaches physicians with the target message, as not only the return of investment (ROI) of each MCM channel must be considered but also its rate of reaching physicians and the quality of the experience (GfK, 2017). The example demonstrates that digital marketing activities are not only evaluated by the traditional ROI model but also by how much they created a valuable experience or engagement with the product or brand, which may lead to a positive brand perception and future prescription intention.

CONCLUSION

Compared to other industries, the pharmaceutical industry, particularly in Korea, tends to adapt digital marketing strategies to their marketing activities more slowly; however, recently enacted strict regulations on pharmaceutical companies have driven pharmaceutical digital marketing. Currently, diverse digital marketing activities are already targeting physicians, and most of them are focusing on providing useful information to clinical physicians in hopes of increasing their promoted products' prescriptions. This essay mostly focused on the current status of pharmaceutical digital marketing activities in Korea; however, how such activities actually affect clinical physicians' practice remains unknown. The unique characteristics of such pharmaceutical marketing activities can be studied for their role as a medical information source for clinical physicians and for their actual influence; however, this area requires more attention from researchers.

References

Article 18 of Medical Service Act, No. 14438 (2016).

Bellman, P., Havens, C., Bertolucci, Y., & Streeter, B. (2005). Facilitating physician access to medical reference information. *Permanente Journal*, 9(4): 27–32.

Bennett, N. L., Casebeer, L. L., Kristofco, R. E., & Strasser, S. M. (2004). Physicians' internet information-seeking behaviors. *Journal of Continuing Education in the Health Professions*, 24(1): 31–38.

Bennett, N. L., Casebeer, L. L., Zheng, S., & Kristofco, R. (2006). Information-seeking behaviors and reflective practice. *Journal of Continuing Education in the Health Professions*, 26(2): 120–127.

Belsey, J. (2007). Advertising and marketing. In Lionel D. Edwards, Adrew J. Fletcher, Anthony W. Fox, & Peter D. Stonier (eds.). *Principles and Practice of Pharmaceutical Medicine* (2nd ed., pp. 653–664).West Sussex, England: John Wiley & Sons Ltd.

Case, Donald O. (2008). 11.1.4. Health Care Providers. *Looking for Information: A Survey of Research on Information Seeking, Needs, and Behavior.* (2nd ed., pp. 265–272). UK: Emerald.

Casebeer, L., Bennett, N., Kristofco, R., Carillo, A., & Centor, R. (2002). Physician internet medical information seeking and on-line continuing education use patterns. *Journal of Continuing Education in the Health Professions*, 22(1): 33–42.

Cha, J. B., Ryu, G. Y., Lee, H. Y. (2013). An Empirical Study on the Relationship Effect of Pharmaceutical Sales Representative's Personal-Job Fit / Person-Organization Fit and Job Satisfaction, Organizational Commitment, and Turnover Intentions. *Korean Journal of Business Administration*, 26(3): 567–588.

Choi, E.T. (2017, December 26th). New government launched, but no public health policy without Moon-care. *Dailiyphram.* Retrived from http://www.dailypharm.com/Users/News/SendNewsPrint.html?mode=print&ID=234951.

Fisher, M.A., Keough, M.E., Baril, J.L., Saccoccio, L., Mazor, K.M., Ladd, E., Worley, A.V., & Gurwitz, J.H. (2009). Prescribers and pharmaceutical representatives: Why are we still meeting?. *Journal of General Internal Medicine*, 24(7): 795–801. doi: 10.1007/s11606-009-0989-6.

Fong, J., Buckley, T., & Cashin, A. (2015). Nurse practitioner prescribing: an international perspective. *Nursing: Research and Reviews*, 5: 99–108, https://doi.org/10.2147/NRR.S56188.

GfK. (2017). *Measuring Multichannel Marketing: Pharma Plays Catch-Up.* Nuremberg, Germany: GfK.

Haug, J. D. (1997). Physicians' preferences for information sources: A meta-analytic study. *Bulletin of the Medical Library Association*, 85(3), 223.

Improper Soliciation and Graft Act, No. 14183 (2016).

James, B. (2004). *An introduction to pharmaceutical marketing.* Retrieved from http://www.scripreports.com

Jang, Y. H. (2017, September 27th). Pharmaceutical marketing also accelerate digitalization. *The Electronic Times*. Retrieved from http://www.etnews.com/20170927000106#

Jung, Y.S., Ahn, S. J., & Yi, H.T. (2017). Differential Effect of Control Mechanism Toward Salesperson on SOCO behaviors and Sales Performance in Pharmaceutical Distribution Channel. *Journal of Distribution Research*, 22(1): 69–91.

Lee, T.S. (2018, January 10th). Pharmaceutical companies strengthening its management of "product launch event," under K-Sunshine Act. Dailypharm. Retrieved from http://www.dailypharm.com/Users/News/SendNewsPrint.html?mode=print&ID=235462

Ministry of Health and Welfare [MOWH]. (2018). *Rebate Double-Impound Policy*. Retrieved From http://www.mohw.go.kr/react/policy/index.jsp?PAR_MENU _ID=06&MENU _ID=06290403&PAGE=3&topTitle=%B8%AE%BA%A3%C0%CC%C6%AE%20% BD%D6%B9%FA%C1%A6

Minnesota Department of Health [MDH]. (2015). A practical guide to electronic prescribing (2nd Ed.). St. Paul, MN: Minnesota Derpartment of Health. Retrieved from http://www.health.state.mn.us/e-health/.

Prosser, H., Almond, S., & Walley, T. (2003). Influence on GP's decision to prescribe new drugs—the importance of who says what. *Family Practice*, 20(1): 61–68.

Song, Yeonju. (2015, September 7th). 5 minute dealers with physicians. Medi:Gate News. Retrieved from http://www.medigatenews.com/news/2019280052

Song, Y.J. (2009). The South Korean health care system. *Japan Medial Association Journal*, 52 (3): 206–209.

Spiller, L. D., & Wymer Jr, W. W. (2001). Physicians' perceptions and uses of commercial drug information sources: An examination of pharmaceutical marketing to physicians. *Health Marketing Quarterly*, 19(1): 91–106.

_____ (2011). Physicians' Responses to Marketing Strategies of Pharmaceutical Companies. *Journal of Pharmaceutical Marketing & Management*, 15(1): 91–106, DOI: 10.3109/ J058v15n01_04.

Squirling, G.K., Mansfield, P.R., Montgomery, B.D., Lexchin, J. Doust, J., Othman, N., & Vitry, A. I. (2010). Information from pharmaceutical companies and the quality, quantity and cost of physicians' prescribing: A systematic review. *PLoS Medicine*, 7(10), e1000352.https://doi.org/10.1371/journal.pmed.1000352

Yi, Ho-Taek (2017). Differential Effect of Salesperson's Personality on Selling Orientation-Customer Orientation and Sales Performance: Focused on Pharmaceutic Distribution Channel. *Journal of Distribution Research*, 22(4): 125–148.

digital
KOREA

Digital Cultures of Financial Advice

Explorations of Online Wealth-Tech Communities in South Korea

6

BOHYEONG KIM

Vanderbilt University

INTRODUCTION

In 2016, a South Korean online forum for lay stock investors called *Chukael*[1] was spotlighted in both popular culture and political affairs. One instance of this coverage was in a Korean television drama entitled *My Wife's Having an Affair This Week* (*JTBC*). Using this real-life online investment forum, the show depicted a man seeking advice on *Chukael* about his wife's alleged affair. It vividly described how the online financial forum was being employed in ways different from what it had been designed for. Whereas *Chukael* was initially created for lay investors to discuss stock investing, it ended up being utilized as a space for nonspecific online chatter including, but not limited to, humor, politics, current affairs, and other trivia. While forum users shared an interest in stock markets, investment talk was no more than one of the various topics discussed. In *My Wife's Having an Affair This Week*, its male lead shared with other *Chukael* users every stage of his experience—from discovering his wife's supposed affair by checking her cell

---

1 It is an abbreviation of Chusik kaellŏri in which chusik means stocks and kaellŏri means "gallery," one of the nouns used more often in referring to online forums in Korea.

phone, to going to a hotel to uncover the affair scene, to being divorced by his wife, and finally to suffering subsequent divorce trauma—which was followed by other fictionalized online users' differing opinions and advice.

Not long after this TV drama aired, the Korean National Assembly held a public grilling over a corruption scandal surrounding President Park Geun-hye and her cronies. While this grilling was aired live on TV and the Internet, a crucial piece of evidence (i.e., a past YouTube clip) was passed from an ordinary citizen to the opposing counsel, which forced one of the most infamous politicians under investigation to admit his involvement. The one who sent the tip-off identified her/himself to be a *Chukael* user ("*chukaeler*") and other *chukaelers* perceived this event as a striking feat by their community. After the grilling, the lawmaker soon posted a photo of herself holding a handwritten thank-you note which ended with a statement that demonstrated the lawmaker's gratitude toward *chukaelers*: "Good luck on your stock investment!"

These two vignettes illustrate how an online forum for stock investing has operated as a *general* forum for broader discussions than those about person-al finance. Interestingly, this aspect has not been limited solely to one specific forum. Rather, a multitude of online financial forums in South Korea have played versatile roles and attracted a diverse group of users. This phenomenon is indicative, above all, of the incorporation of "investment talk" into the everyday realm of digital culture, as well as the incorporation of laypeople into the financial investment world. Since a particular point in history, everyday individuals—not solely market professionals or financial elites—have gathered and continue to gather around online financial forums. Defining the prevalence of online financial communities as a signal of the "Financialization of daily life" (Martin, 2002) in South Korea, this chapter provides an overview of the history of online financial communities and the ways they have taken shape on a wide spectrum of commodification.

Based on local terminology, the emphasis of this chapter will be on what is called "wealth-tech." As a translation of the Korean word *chaeteku*, wealth-tech refers to the techniques of personal finance and money-management, mostly through investing in stocks, funds, real estate and other financial products (Kim, 2017). Emulating *"zeiteku"*—a buzzword within Japan's business circles in the second half of the 1980s (Kikkawa, 2012)—Korean journalists introduced the neologism *"chaeteku"* to the Korean public in the 1980s. By the mid-1990s the word became familiar, at least, to newspaper readers.

After going through the Asian Financial Crisis, and in tandem with the development of the Internet and the flowering of digital cultures, those who were interested in wealth-tech began to actively utilize digital channels. This chapter presents an overview of such digital culture of wealth-tech with a focus on online wealth-tech communities. In doing so, this chapter has relied on online and offline observations, archival data, and in-depth interviews with users.

THE RISE OF ONLINE WEALTH-TECH COMMUNITIES IN THE POST-"IMF CRISIS" ERA

Wealth-tech has been a popular topic in the online exchange of information since the era of PC communications.[2] When rudimentary forms of virtual communities on various PC communications platforms became popular in the mid-1990s, lay investors ventured online to discuss trading strategies. Prior to PC communications, newspapers had been the main source from which lay investors acquired wealth-tech information. They also utilized consumer education (i.e., investment seminars) offered by the industry (e.g., brokerage firms, financial media corporations, "cultural centers" of department stores). For these everyday investors, the birth of online communities indicated that they no longer had to rely on such top-down, commercial undertakings to gather financial information; moreover, they now had an easier way to organize groups of like-minded people.

2 PC communication services enabled users to network with each other via a text-based interface by using a keyboard, a modem as well as telephone lines (Lee, 2016). Commercial PC communications services (e.g., *Chollian, Hitel*) first arrived in Korean homes in 1988, leading to South Korea witnessing the emergence of a network-based digital culture.

It was during the early 2000s when the number of online wealth-tech communities skyrocketed. Freechal, a then popular portal site, by July 2003 had hosted more than 160 wealth-tech communities; then the number of wealth-tech communities across different online platforms reached 3,000 only three months later (*Herald Business*, July 21, 2003; *Seoul Shinmun*, October 29, 2003). A close observation of Daum—one of the nation's leading portal sites—indicates that the number of its wealth-tech cafés[3] increased by around 7,040% in 13 years, 2003–2016.

The number significantly increases when we examine similar cafés within other subcategories. For instance, Daum places wealth-tech cafés under an umbrella category called "Economy/Finance," which in turn is subdivided into "Real Estate," "Securities," "Insurance," and others in addition to "Wealth-tech." The Economy/Finance category shows 257,717 cafés as of 2018, thereby demonstrating an increase by 247 percent from 104,483 in 2008 (*Maeil Business Newspaper*, February 20, 2008). Some wealth-tech cafés cover a multitude of different pathways to wealth-tech (i.e., stocks, funds, bonds, real estate) while others focus on a specific genre of wealth-tech (e.g., real estate auctions).

The Asian Financial Crisis (or the "IMF crisis") of 1997 laid the groundwork for the burgeoning of online wealth-tech communities. With the IMF crisis, South Korea witnessed a new mode of capitalist production, deregulation of financial markets, and neoliberal social governing (Chang, 2016; C. Choi, 2016; Song, 2009, 2011). With their witnessing of massive layoffs, underemployment, and involuntary early retirement, those who previously had achieved upward mobility through wage work began to turn their eyes to finance.

The IMF crisis was also crucial in producing digital subjectivities in South Korea. ICTs were called on to resolve the crisis in addition to other restructuring measures. With close ties to emerging neoliberal discourses such as flexibilization and self-development, desirable digital subjects appeared to be

---

3 The term "café," which once used to refer to the online-community platform developed by Daum, has become a general term referring to an online community itself.

Figure 1. The number of wealth-tech cafés on Daum

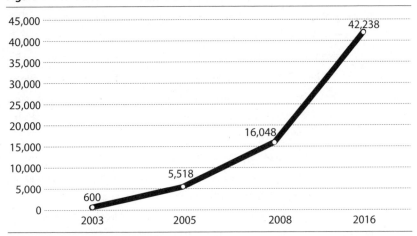

Sources: *Hankyung Business*, Aug 7, 2005; *Maeil Business Newspaper*, February 20, 2008.

those "who are conscientious and self-sufficient citizens" of a depoliticized digital space (Yang, 2017: 744). In other words, the capability to navigate digital spaces was construed as necessary for one to be an autonomous, self-improving citizen, which was deemed ideal for the new economy. Online wealth-tech communities came to epitomize the merging of this neoliberal ethos and digital cultures.

Some wealth-tech cafés grew into some of the most popular cafés across all variety of topics. Café Ten in Ten (http://cafe.daum.net/10in10) is one such big-time wealth-tech café. Created in June 2001 on Daum, it became so popular that its slogan "ten in ten" (transliterated into *t'enint'en*)—an abbreviation for "Making Ten *eok* won [roughly $900,000 USD] in Ten years"—was selected as one of the Words of the Year in 2004 by the National Institute of the Korean Language. Its members rapidly increased as they sought each other's opinions about household accounting, wealth-tech plans, investment portfolios, and spending habits.

As of May 2016, Café Ten in Ten had more than 822 thousand members, more than 302 million hits, 2.4 million posts, and 10.4 million comments, as well as more than 100 thousand daily visitors. It indeed has become today

Figure 2. The number of Café Ten in Ten members (in thousands)

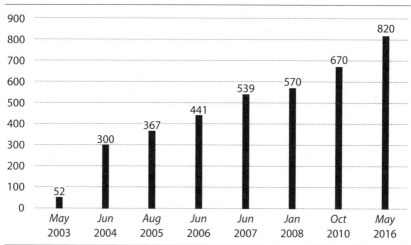

Sources: *Hankook Ilbo*, May 22, 2003; *Herald Business*, November 24, 2003; *Financial News*, June 13, 2004; *Edaily*, February 20, 2007; *Maeil Business Economy*, February 20, 2008; *Luxmen*, October, 2010.

one of the top-ranked cafés among millions of Daum cafés. In terms of membership, Café Ten in Ten has brought together people from diverse backgrounds and circumstances. They range from married to divorced to single; from successful to struggling; from entrepreneurs to housewives to the unemployed; from financial professionals to white-collar workers to blue-collar laborers to students. According to descriptive statistics posted by its moderator in 2009, 54% of users were female and 46% male. In terms of age, 22% were in their twenties, 45% in their thirties, 19% in their forties, and finally 8% in their fifties or over.

　　Café Ten in Ten was made visible in the mass media from its earliest phase. While its founder-cum-moderator pursued media attention, the growing fields of financial journalism and online media were also in need of content to fill their pages or airtime. Online wealth-tech communities, saturated with personal narratives of financial management and mutual advice among lay people, were great sources for financial media which were seeking out lay audiences. Therefore, online wealth-tech communities and financial journalism grew into a complicit relationship to ensure their growth. For example, Daum, a commercial portal site which also operated as a media platform displaying news content, expanded its financial advice section in 2004 to capitalize on the content produced by Café Ten in Ten users. It curated popular posts from Café Ten in Ten under the heading "Make ten *eok* won in ten years."

In the same year, a major economic paper, *Maeil Business Newspaper*, launched a get-rich campaign in collaboration with Café Ten in Ten. Its company organized wealth-tech lectures for Café Ten in Ten members that in turn were covered in the newspaper. In fact, this collaborative relation has been ongoing. One example of such collaboration is the newspaper's special promotion offered for Café Ten in Ten members: a year-long subscription of a business magazine published by the same company at a discounted price. Moreover, this magazine has been freely circulated to participants at offline events organized by the Café. This symbiotic relationship has helped the financial media company widen their readership on the one hand and the Café to establish its legitimation on the other. Other newspaper companies, securities firms, banks as well as financial services companies have also offered wealth-tech lectures for members of Café Ten in Ten since the early 2000s.

The number of wealth-tech cafés on Daum greatly increased in 2007 when investment (especially in funds) boomed until the global economic crisis broke out in 2008. Between January 2007 and January 2008 the number of cafés in the Economy/Finance category increased by 76 percent, from 79,885 to 104,483. Furthermore, the number of cafés under its three subcategories (real estate, securities, and wealth-tech) increased by 233 percent in three years, from around 18,000 in 2005 to 42,000 in 2008. The number of Café Ten in Ten's members also increased by thirty percent between 2006 and 2008. A 2008 newspaper article reported that Café Ten in Ten ranked the 15th among 6.5 million Daum cafés (*Maeil Business Newspaper*, February 20, 2008).

A TWO-TRACK STRATEGY OF ONLINE WEALTH-TECH CAFÉS

Online financial communities help lay people access the information and resources necessary for successful investment, which in turn makes financial markets (especially stock markets) more accessible to them. In this respect, online financial communities have been described as spaces of collective sensemaking (Bourne, 2017; Herrmann, 2007) or "tribal spaces" where information and trading strategies are shared as gifts (Campbell et al., 2009). However, most online wealth-tech communities demonstrate traits of self-organizing as well as those of commodification of financial information. In other words, many of them lie on a continuum in-between voluntariness at one end and commodification at the other. This spectrum was created when market professionals in the financial advice sector strove to utilize online communities for their business arrangements while lay investors have grown wary of for-profit wealth-tech advice. In general, wealth-tech markets are fraught with uncertainty, deception, rumor, and failure. While wealth-tech advice has forged an enormous enterprise, much of it has been linked with sales of financial products, highly expensive stock-selection services, and real estate brokerages (Kim, 2017: 614). Therefore, online wealth-tech communities in response have developed a sense of resistance against the establishment with many of their members aspiring to become autonomous investors. Consequently, many of the popular wealth-tech cafés which have recruited a high number of members were created by non-professionals.

For example, when Café Ten in Ten was created in 2001, its moderator was an obscure white-collar worker whose occupation had nothing to do with wealth-tech advice. As his café became famous and his financial investments on the long-term horizon turned a profit, he left his job and launched an offline, paid wealth-tech seminar. This online community therefore has operated broadly in two different ways: 1) opening up a free, online forum where like-minded people share their interests in wealth-tech, and 2) functioning as a gateway into a paid, in-person wealth-tech seminar. By bringing together different investment strategies, experience, knowledge, and skills from a diverse group of people, users dig deep into the world of wealth-tech, whether it be stocks, funds, real estate, or other topics. If they are interested in taking an offline class, they can sign up for a fee-based seminar. Other commercial activities (e.g., promoting financial products, advertising from third-parties, paid seminars) are highly restricted.

In terms of the first mode of operation—like-minded people sharing their interests in wealth-tech—Café Ten in Ten users wrote about their specific difficulties and financial situations (i.e., income, expenses, spending habits, assets, goals) while other members gave feedback. The following post and comment from Café Ten in Ten users exemplify how its members made use of online wealth-tech communities in ways that allowed them to freely exchange concerns and advice on personal finance:

> My goal is making 100 million won ($90,000 dollars) in five years. I will start my first job soon. My annual salary will be around 24 million won ($21,600 dollars). My monthly income will be 1.5 million won ($1,350 dollars) in usual months and 2.5 million won ($2,250 dollars) in bonus months. Previously, I received the same amount of money from my parents every month. So, I don't know how to manage fluctuating monthly salaries in terms of installment savings. . . . Please share with me how much working professionals spend in general, what kind wealth-tech products are good for them, and how they use installment savings plans. (Online post, September 1, 2002)

Responding to this post, a user revealed her or his portfolio and suggested the following:

> . . . If you're really determined, I'd like to suggest this:
> — A savings plan for lower-income employees [*kŭnlocha utae chŏ ch'uk*]: 500,000 won ($450 dollars). The highest interest rates at 8.5% in the non-banking sector; this year is the last year for this tax exemption.
> — A savings plan specifically for housing [*chutaek bugŭm*]: 135,000 won ($121.50 dollars). This amount of monthly contribution allows you to be prioritized when bidding on new condominiums in Seoul in

two years.

— 1 year time deposit [*chŏngki yekŭm*]: 1 million won ($900 dollars). The highest interest rates at 7% in the non-banking sector; with tax benefits. (Online post, September 1, 2002)

Such practices of advice-sharing illustrate the widely-researched traits found to be prevalent among digital cultures, such as voluntary participation, altruism and generosity (e.g., Green & Jenkins, 2009).

The discussion now turns to the second mode by which online wealth-tech cafés function: that of gateways into fee-based, "in the flesh" wealth-tech seminars. In 2009, the founder-cum-moderator of Café Ten in Ten launched his Ten in Ten Academy (hereafter "the Academy"), his first effort in offering in-person, for-profit seminars. The Academy, consisting of five weekly 3-hour lectures, taught how to become rich, why wealth-tech is necessary along with financial literacy and "investment 101" (see Kim 2017 for a detailed analysis of the program). It is important to note that only one out of thirty-six bulletin boards[4] within Café Ten in Ten has been devoted to promoting the Academy. Its founder-cum-moderator has run the Academy on his own. In this respect, he has played two significantly different roles within the café: a moderator of the free, online community on the one hand and an entrepreneur of a paid program on the other. By leaving most spaces of Café Ten in Ten for voluntary discussions by users, he is notably distinguishable from global financial gurus (e.g., Robert Kiyosaki, Suze Orman) who command their own websites as part of their multi-platform marketing (Lee, 2012; Zaloom, 2016).

Over the past decade, approximately 15,000 people have participated in the Ten in Ten Academy. Participants have been diverse in terms of gender, class, and age, but many have been white-collar workers in their thirties and forties. Its operator—that is, the moderator-cum-founder of Café Ten in

---

4 Each café can have multiple bulletin boards; in keeping with this trend, Café Ten in Ten has created a variety of bulletin boards. Some bulletin boards are focused on a specific category of investing (e.g., stocks, funds, real estate).

Ten—once noted that the average age of participants was 37. Fifty to sixty people taking the seminar concurrently have made up each "cohort" of the program and some of them have continued to network even after their five-week program ended. The program changed its name to the "Economic Freedom Academy" in mid 2016. More importantly, a significant change was made to its enrollment fee. Its operator had boasted about the afford-ability of the program, contrasting its alleged inexpensive fee with other quasi rip-off wealth-tech seminars. However, whereas its enrollment fee remained relatively affordable for a long time, it was increased twice over the span of six years (from 100,000 won or $90 dollars in 2012 to 200,000 won or $180 dollars in 2018).

Since late 2016, Café Ten in Ten has expanded its offline programs by adding other one-time lectures. Presenting this series as "Lectures for Sharing" [*nanum kangŭi*], the stated goal has been to provide café users with quality wealth-tech lectures at an affordable price (10,000 won or $9 dol-lars). Mostly taught by wealth-tech authors, lectures have been offered on an array of topics that are mostly related to wealth-tech but some cover non-financial topics as well.

This "two-track" strategy—on the one hand leaving an online space as a voluntary association and on the other providing interested users with off-line, for-fee programs—has been adopted by other wealth-tech advisors who have stepped up to take advantage of the opportunity to make extra money through teaching the art of moneymaking. Café Happy Wealth-tech (http://cafe.daum.net/happy-tech) illustrates how latecomers followed suit. Whereas Café Ten in Ten has covered all topics related to wealth-tech, Café Happy Wealth-tech has been focused on real estate investments, especially property auctions. Its moderator had been one of Café Ten in Ten's colum-nists; Café Ten in Ten had a number of designated columnists who actively shared their real-world investment tips. Numerous columnists have become big names within Café Ten Ten over the past fifteen years and many of them have established a reputation as wealth-tech experts and/or authors. The moderator of Café Happy Wealth-tech is one of them and he ended up run-ning his own wealth-tech café on Daum.

Created in 2008, Café Happy Wealth-tech has 232,749 members and fifty different bulletin boards as of February 2018. Members are allowed to post on most of the bulletin boards to share their experience, tips, strategies, and questions regarding real estate investments. At the same time, similar to Café Ten in Ten, Café Happy Wealth-tech has had specific boards where only designated members have been allowed to publish their advice columns. Also, a significant part of using this café has involved taking various offline real-estate investment classes for which members have had to sign up through the café.

Whereas Café Ten in Ten's offline course was limited for a long time to the Academy, Café Happy Wealth-tech's offline classes have been more expansive from its early stage. As of early 2018, it offers nine different classes on a regular basis—all related to real estate investments but each class has a different focus. The following is a list of the nine regular courses: Real Estate Auctions (Basic, Intermediate, Upper-Intermediate & Advanced), Investing in Commercial Buildings (Basic & Advanced), Value Investing in Real Estate, Redevelopment/Rebuilding, and Renting out Homes. Most programs are broken down into four to six weeks (three hour per each week) and the enrollment fee ranges from 360,000 won ($342 dollars) to 450,000 won ($405 dollars). In addition to its moderator, faculty is made up of other bestselling authors in the field of real estate investment. Similar to the Ten in Ten Academy, participants of each offline program have formed their cohort groups for networking.

Members of Café Happy Wealth-tech have been free to choose either to utilize the free, online space only or to take offline classes. In addition to the nine regular classes, Café Happy Wealth-tech has offered various special one-time lectures. It has been so competitive that when one signs up for special lectures most of these lectures have been sold out in less than an hour. Because of the two-track strategy, online wealth-tech communities operate as a revenue stream for successful investors while, at the same time, they enable everyday investors to network in-person with one another. Because most lay people consider investment to be challenging, networking with other investors has been regarded as crucial in gathering information and

managing risks. Many users of online wealth-tech communities make use of
the two tracks depending on their interests and availability.

Mijung[5] (48, female, a retail cashier, interviewed on November 11, 2014)
joined Café Ten in Ten in the early 2000s. She became interested in investment after her husband was laid off during the height of the IMF crisis.
Television programs on a business cable introduced her to the financial
world and online wealth-tech communities.[6] Following a pundit on TV,
Mijung looked up the online community that he created and it became the
very first wealth-tech café that she joined. Once introduced to the field of
online wealth-tech communities, it was easy for her to discover Café Ten in
Ten, which was at the center of wealth-tech buzzwords in the early 2000s.
Although she had shopped around various wealth-tech communities for several years, it was not until 2007 that she ventured into the act of investing.
Her first investment was in mutual funds partly because they had the lowest
threshold compared to stocks or real estate. From time to time, she had participated in offline meetups organized within various online wealth-tech
communities. Finally, Mijung ended up taking the Ten in Ten Academy in
2014—almost a decade after she had joined Café Ten in Ten; since participating in the Academy, she has invested her capital into real estate markets.

While Mijung's footsteps show one's transformation from an online *participant* to a *consumer* of financial advice to a full-fledged *investor*, the experience of Beomyoung (42, male, a white-collar employee) demonstrates that
the ways people utilize online and offline perks of wealth-tech communities
can vary. He was a newcomer to Café Ten in Ten, but registered for its offline seminar even before he got to familiarize himself with its online space.
In order to make use of one of his employee benefits—reimbursement for

---

5 Pseudonyms are used to protect the anonymity of research participants.
6 Financial media companies expanded their business into cable channels after the 1990s.
  For example, the *Maeil Business Newspaper* company launched a financial business television channel, *MBN*, in March 1995. Another prominent financial paper, *Korea Business
  News*, launched its cable TV channel in 2000. In addition to providing stock market
  analysis and investment advice, such business channels aired a financial literacy program
  and offered customized wealth-tech advice for a fee.

book purchases—he looked up bestselling books; the first in the search results was a Café Ten in Ten post. His click on the post invited him to the
whole new world of wealth-tech. Mesmerized by the expansive amount of
information on moneymaking, he enrolled for the Academy in the second
that its promotion post captured his eyes. I first met him at an after-party of
the Ten in Ten Academy during its first week. By the time we rejoined in
four weeks, he became much more knowledgeable about financial jargon by
reading through Café Ten in Ten, wealth-tech blogs, and books. His discovery of Café Ten in Ten and participation in the Academy changed his
lifestyle in only four weeks. Through an intensive self-study, Beomyoung
now felt somewhat confident to the extent that he wanted to offer his own
opinions for those who sought out investment advice.

Beomyoung shared with me the lessons that he took away from his research: "The bottom line is that in capitalist society money is filial piety,
money is sibling affection, and money is happiness" (Interview, March 22,
2015). Yet the act of reading was not enough for him to attain these virtues
which he associated with money. Therefore he contacted one of the colum-
nists on Café Ten in Ten who specialized in real estate. He also began to
look up other wealth-tech seminars and started his own wealth-tech blog. In
addition, he set a new year's resolution: to become a wealth-tech lecturer
himself. His experience represents the process in which an individual transformed himself—via the use of online wealth-tech communities—from a
wage worker to a self-entrepreneurial investor subject.

MAKING DETOURS UNDER THE COMMODIFICATION OF
ONLINE WEALTH-TECH COMMUNITIES

The most commodified form of online wealth-tech communities funnel
their emphasis to for-fee services which involve the selection of stocks or
properties. While the aforementioned cafés commodified their online "communities" by selling seminars and lectures, these programs still advocated for
the autonomy of lay investors. For example, the programs offered by Café

Ten in Ten or Café Happy Wealth-tech highlighted the need to develop one's own ability to analyze markets, select valuable investment items and manage a risk. In contrast, the more commodified online "communities" were no more than a marketing platform for their wealth-tech brokerage services.

Sunny (44, female, a casual laborer) bought a home through a court auction, for the sake of making cash by renting out its rooms. She chose which house to bid on by relying entirely on a wealth-tech advisor whose class she was taking. The advisor was running a wealth-tech café on Daum, which he primarily used as an advertising platform for his real-estate seminars. Its fee, 800,000 won ($720 dollars) for eight 3 hour-long lectures, was much higher than those of the aforementioned programs. Sunny nonetheless affirmed: "It's expensive if you think it's just a lecture fee. But it's inexpensive if you think it includes payments for networking" (interview on March 26, 2015). By taking the wealth-tech advisor's class, Sunny was able to solicit his opinion on the properties that she was checking out in the auction market. After all, the advisor strongly recommended a particular property and advised on its bidding price. She bought it at 230 million won ($207,000 dollars) with 70 percent of bank loans. In this case, an online community was the means by which a brokerage service was promoted in the name of financial advice.

Given such a wide spectrum of commodification of online wealth-tech "communities," one of my research participants (Sunwoo, 49, male, a retired fund manager)—who was participating in an array of online wealth-tech communities and their offline events—divided them into three different types according to the extent of commodification. The first type was the most commodified one, which offered a seminar as a *lure* into for-pay services. The second type manifested a true sense of community by fostering deep "feelings of fellowship" [*tongnyu ŭisik*]. This type encouraged its members to march together for economic freedom. The third type existed in-between the first and the second types, prodding users to learn and practice wealth-tech on their own but at the same time making paid services available upon request (conversation with Sunwoo on September 15, 2014).

Many users of online wealth-tech communities were wary of such aspects of commodification across online and offline realms. While some users like Sunny accepted the commodification as inevitable and even beneficial, other users actively sought for a detour or alternative. Organizing a study group was one way to evade or minimize commercial influences on their effective wealth-tech practices. For example, Sunwoo was leading a wealth-tech study group which was made up of former participants in the Ten in Ten Academy. One of its members was familiar with real estate auctioning and another was a very successful stock investor. The novice study group members appreciated the quality information which these experienced investors taught them for free. In one study meeting, Sunwoo, a former market professional, shared his observation that since the real estate market was stumbling investors were turning their eyes to private lectures instead of their own investment activities.

Jun (36, male, a medical laboratory technologist) was more aggressive in avoiding having to pay for services in his discovery of potentially profitable properties. He joined a real-estate investment café that was focused only on small-size condos. He read all the advice posts written by its moderator within two weeks and he came to buy into the rationale behind why a small-size condo was the best investment item. For brokerage services, the café moderator posted specifics of each property that he found to be profitable, but with its real name and/or address hidden. One had to pay around $2,700 dollars to the moderator-cum-broker if one wanted to acquire the actual address of each property. Since Jun was finding the broker fees to be unreasonable and he was having difficulties in determining on his own which properties were valuable, he began to track down the actual properties which the moderator-cum-broker had posted. Even with incomplete information, he was able to narrow down the offerings to several apartment complexes in a particular neighborhood and then to call nearby realtors. After a couple of successes, his detective techniques developed:

> This guy was focused on a few small cities and I came to learn such-and-such specifics usually fall into such-and-such neighborhoods. And when I wanted to confirm, I called realtors. Because this guy usually

reveals the property's square foot, floor, and the price, when I ask the realtor, 'Hey, do you have such-and-such apartment for sales?' Then the realtor says 'yes'. And there could be some liabilities on the property. If I ask about liabilities, the realtor say, 'Yes, that's right.' It means I've found it! (Interview on November 12, 2014).

While numerous online wealth-tech "communities" take advantage of on-line community platforms, many of them are practically nothing but web-sites for financial services. This indicates not only that financial information has been commodified in digital spaces, but also that *online communities* themselves have become commodified. Nonetheless, many users have con-tested commodification in different ways in their pursuits of wealth-tech.

CONCLUSION

While financial journalism and infotainment have played a central role in producing the mass investment culture in the West (Chakravartty & Schiller, 2010; Clark, Thrift & Tickell, 2004), online wealth-tech communities have played as crucial a role in spreading the cultures of finance in South Korea. The prevalence of online wealth-tech communities is not solely concomitant to the financialization of the Korean economy; rather, it has been integral to the process in terms of its significant contribution to the normalization of investing and to the incorporation of a lay audience into financial capitalism. Moreover, it is particularly valuable to understand the rise of online wealth-tech communities in relation not only to the economic restructuring that occurred after the IMF crisis, but also to the merging of a neoliberal ethos with digital cultures.

References

Bourne, C. D. (2017). Sensemaking in an online community after financial loss: Enterprising Jamaican investors and the fall of a financial messiah. *New Media & Society*, 19(6): 843–860.

Campbell, J., Fletcher, G., & Greenhill, A. (2009). Conflict and identity shape shifting in an online financial community. *Information Systems Journal*, 19(5): 461–478.

Chang, K.-S. (2016). Financialization of poverty: Proletarian financial crisis in post-developmental Korea. *Research in Political Economy*, 31: 109–134.

Choi, C. (2016). *The cultural political economy of financialization in South Korea after the Asian Financial Crisis: The financial subsumption of individuals and households*. Doctoral dissertation. Chung-Ang University. (in Korean)

Choi, M. (2011). *Financialization of daily life and the making of investor subject after 1997 economic crisis in Korea*. MA thesis. Seoul National University. (in Korean)

Clark, G. L., Thrift, N., & Tickell, A. (2004). Performing finance: the industry, the media and its image. *Review of International Political Economy*, 11(2): 289–310.

Green, J., & Jenkins, H. (2009). The moral economy of web 2.0. In J. Holt and A. Perren (eds.). *Media Industries History, Theory, and Method* (pp. 213–225), Malden, MA: Willey-Blackwell.

Herrmann, A. F. (2007). Stockholders in cyberspace: Weick's sensemaking online. *Journal of Business Communication*, 44(1): 13–35.

Kikkawa, T. (2012). Tragedy of the Nouveau Rich: Encountered by the Japanese Economy, Based on the post-war history of financial system. Available at: http://hermes-ir.lib. hitu.ac.jp/rs/bitstream/10086/22917/3/070hibsWP_140.pdf (accessed April 2, 2014).

Kim, B. (2017). Think rich, feel hurt: the critique of capitalism and the production of affect in the making of financial subjects in South Korea. *Cultural Studies*, 31(5): 611–633.

Lee, K.-S. (2016). On the historiography of the Korean Internet: Issues raised by the historical dialectic of structure and agency. *The Information Society*, 32(3): 217–222.

Lee, M. (2012). A feminist political economic critique of women and investment in the popular media. *Feminist Media Studies*, 14(2): 270–285.

Martin, R. (2002). *Financialization of Daily Life*. Philadelphia: Temple University Press.

Song, J. (2009). *South Koreans in the Debt Crisis: The Creation of a Neoliberal Welfare Society*. Durham: Duke University Press.

_____ (2014). *Living on Your Own: Single Women, Rental Housing, and Post-Revolutionary Affect in Contemporary South Korea*. Albany: SUNY Press.

_____ (ed.) (2011). *New Millennium South Korea: Neoliberal Capitalism and Transnational Movements*. Routledge.

Yang, S. (2017). Networking South Korea: Internet, nation, and new subjects. *Media, Culture & Society*, 39(5): 740–749.

Zaloom, C. (2016). The evangelical financial ethic: Doubled forms and the search for God in the economic world. *American Ethnologist*, 43(2): 325–338.

digital
KOREA

Digitalization, Labor Flexibility and the Change of Cultural Production in the Korean Broadcasting Industry

7

CHANGWOOK KIM

Handong Global University

Since the late 1990s, much academic and public attention has addressed the success in East and Southeast Asian markets of Korean popular culture, widely known as the Korean Wave. This rapid dissemination of Korean popular culture throughout Asian markets has changed our understanding of Korean cultural industries. In Korea itself, the wave has stimulated continuous governmental support of these cultural industries as an evolving economic sector. Moreover, in scholarship and media coverage we can trace the dominance of creative industry discourse that has envisioned these Korean industries as generating innovation and optimum employment (e,g., Yeo, 2006; Hankook KyungJae, 2010). The increasing global circulation and consumption of Korean cultural content offer the opportunity to examine the emergence of East Asia as the site of new regional cultural flows in opposition to "Western" cultural production's unidirectional hegemony (e,g., Huat & Iwabuchi, 2008; Jin, 2007). This state-driven developmentalist strategy has been seen as a model for other nations' cultural industries in the context of globalization (Evans, 1995, Chosun Ilbo, 2010).

※ This chapter is revised and developed from "Labor and the limits of seduction in Korea's Creative Economy," *Television & New Media*, 15: 562 (2014).

Contrary to their substantial attention on the consumption and circulation of Korean cultural products, scholars have focused less on the production side of this equation. This chapter will begin to fill this gap by addressing three inter-related questions: (1) How does the legacy of Korea's developmentalist state shape the terms of the national cultural industry? (2) What are the production system's specific institutional features within this cultural industry? and more importantly, (3) How does digitalization change the labor process in this industry? To examine these questions, this study explores the independent television production sector which epitomizes current changes in Korea's cultural industry in terms of greater global integration after the 1997 economic crisis, increasing commercialization, and digitalization. This sector is a fitting subject by which to analyze how local understanding of the discourse of global cultural industry transforms its production regime and what are the implications for its workers. This sector emerged as a result of not only a shift away from a public network broadcasting model, but also the passage of the 1991 "compulsory television programming outsourcing policy." The latter regulatory change is an explicit example of how the Korean government responded at the 'local' level to global pressures which advocated for neo-liberal reform. I argue that independent production (here below IP) sector workers are representative of state-promoted externalization as well as flexible program production. This study will examine these labor processes in the broadcasting sector to assess how a "globalized" local cultural industry potentially changes its production practices and how this process impacts on its workers. After locating my argument within debates about labor within media and cultural studies, I will turn to explore the emerging digitalized flexible production regime and its influences on the IP sector workers by using the concept of labor flexibility.

KOREAN BROADCASTING IN THE ERA OF GLOBALIZATION

After a lengthy military rule, political democratization in the 1990s coin-
cided with a turn toward neo-liberal economic reforms. Korea's 1987 democratic turmoil provided the momentum to transform Korea's development
state from "strong and repressive" to "limited or flexible" to "market-driven"
(Lee, 2009). In terms of broadcasting policy, distinctive differences between
a strong state-driven policy on the one hand and market-driven policy on
the other can be understood by comparing key policies passed under each
political regime. The Chun Doo-Whan administration (1980–1988) implemented the eorontongpaehap, "compulsory reform of the media," that forced
state-owned broadcasters and pro-government newspapers to merge competing private broadcast channels and private local newspapers, ultimately
repressing press freedom. This explicit example demonstrates how a strong
regime controlled content and ownership within the national media industry.

In contrast to this politically-repressive measure, the Kim Young-Sam
administration (1993–1998), as the first civilian government, implemented
pro-market media policies with the initiation of Segyehwa in which the
developing state actively encouraged globalization to respond to external
pressures from U.S. and global institutions (Ryoo, 2008); Segyehwa differs
from neoliberals' views in that it not only interprets globalization as simply
economic liberalization but also defines far more comprehensive political,
cultural and social projects involving the cooperation of local capitals and
civil society (Ryoo, 2008: 878). During this period, the national broadcasting industry underwent dramatic commercialization (Shim, 2006) with
the start-up of commercial cable TV and four new regional commercial ter-
restrial television stations. The government also promoted the bangsong
hoejujungchak, the "compulsory television programming outsourcing policy,"
that required network broadcasters to air a certain number of programs produced by IP companies. This "outsourcing policy" of a "flexible and limited
state" has been critiqued as stemming from an 'immature' local understanding of corporate, liberal ideas of broadcasting (Shim, 2006). For example, the government argued that competition stimulates the 'natural'

development of program diversity in order to promote democracy. Competition through commercialization thus became a dominant strategy for guaranteeing democracy and for enhancing the 'global competitive power of Korea's national cultural industries (Youn & Jang, 2002).

Under the new market-driven state policy regime in the name of "globalization," the vertical production practice led by giant broadcast networks (e.g., *KBS* and *MBC*) turned to the IP sector for more flexible production terms, and this production regime transformation influenced its labor market. Because of the outsourcing program ratio's increase in network broadcasting, the number of IP companies and workers increased dramatically;[2] these numbers are expected to grow, likely changing the entire labor market structure of the Korean broadcasting industry. Despite job growth, workers entering this market face excessive competition; most IP companies are small and ill-equipped in terms of workforce, facilities and financial backing (Shim, 2006).

Young workers entering this field perceive jobs that are associated with "immaterial labor" as 'liberal,' 'creative,' and 'attractive' (Qiu & Kim, 2010). Along with this social recognition, most universities over the past decade have instituted communication, journalism and related departments. Likewise, the number of media-related educational institutions has dramatically expanded, so that the future academic workforce exceeds job demand, as

---

2 The external production program ratio in broadcasting networks reached nearly 30% of their total programming, while the number of IP companies increased almost five-fold from 115 in 1998 to 551 in 2005 (KOBACO, 2005), leading to labor market changes within the Korean broadcasting industry. In 2004, 8,005 workers were in IP companies, representing 56.6% of network broadcast workers and 82.7% of cable TV workers (KOBACO, 2005). Despite this increasing trend, most IP companies suffer from difficult industrial conditions. According to a 2005 KOBACO report on IP companies, the average capital of these companies was $500,000 in 2004. 70% of the sampled companies could be classified as small and medium-sized enterprises because their average capital was below $300,000. The average number of workers per company was 14, with 77.7 % producing cultural and documentary programs for the networks. Most leading IP companies are managed by ex-network broadcasting staff members with personal connections to network broadcasters (KOBACO, 2005).

governmental reports indicate (KBI, 2002). However, it is well-known that procuring high-income and secure jobs in major network broadcasting has become unrealistic for most entrants: only a few job openings exist based on stiff exams, due to network broadcastings' financial constraints after the IMF crisis, part of the 1997 Asian Financial crisis (KBI, 2004). This crisis influenced major broadcasters to cut budgets due to decreasing advertising revenues. Over this period, three network broadcasters reduced airtime and foreign program imports as cost-cutting strategies (Jin, 2007). By contrast, network broadcasters strategically used IP companies because their general-outsourced production costs were far less than network production costs (Jin, 2007). Because of this increase in outsourcing practices, large-scale employment restructuring—derived from labor externalization and flexibility—was implemented in major network broadcasting during this crisis (KBI, 2004). One can predict growth in the flow of labor supply into this rising independent sector because the network keeps their highly selective employment practices based on rigid apprenticeships marked by gender hierarchies: fulltime male program directors and contingent female script-writers (Kim, 2005).

LABOR IN THE GLOBAL CREATIVE ECONOMY

Several theoretical approaches on understanding labor within globalized cultural industries provide useful starting-points. Firstly, political economic approaches highlight forms of 'new exploitation' within these industries from a macro-industrial viewpoint (e,g. Day, 2007; Sullivan, 2007; Mosco & Steven, 2007; Miller et al. 2005). Christopherson (2008) examines how de-regulation, media supply expansion and technological innovations within U.S. cultural industries exacerbate the gap between core and peripheral workers; this process illustrates that the disruption of established professional and craft identities resulting from such technological turns may solidify the position of white males within dominant "hard-wired" social and economic networks, thereby reducing employers' worries about risk while simultaneously segmenting the labor force in terms of gender and race.

In contrast to political economic approach, the ethnographic study of cultural labor aims to follow the daily experiences of media workers by using qualitative methods of participant observation and in-depth interviews. Despite industry's difficult labor conditions—characterized by excessive work hours, unstable employment terms, and relatively lower wages—people willingly enter this market because the jobs enable them to pursue new labor subjectivity, such as "self-expression" and "self-exploration," that are related to their emotional pleasure (e.g., McRobbie, 2016). Ursell (2000) refers to this cultural work as "a seductive vampire," embodying both structural exploitation and the effects of postindustrial society's erotic power. Hesmondhalgh and Baker (2008) uncover some seemingly hidden factors that influence cultural workers' subjectivity, such as "emotional rules of production," referring to their tendency to place themselves within the labor process.

To sum up, previous research about cultural work has examined the territory for generating new modalities of production and exploitation as well as new labor ethics and subjectivities that are aligned with the needs of contemporary capitalism. To better capture historically specific as well as contradictory dimensions of creative labor, this study attempts to offer both a structural and organizational analysis of labor conditions. In particular, this study suggests to explain the organizational characteristics of IP sector by using the concept of labor "flexibility". In the next section, I will briefly explain the concept of labor flexibility, and then, drawing from secondary research, policy reports and qualitative interviews, this study will focus on how the structural aspects of labor processes—such as organizational forms, labor conditions and work practices—change under a digitalized flexible production regime. I undertook in-depth interviews and participant observation in 2007, 2008 and 2017, with 36 IP workers in Seoul, including program directors (PDs), scriptwriters, technicians and managers.[3]

---

3 I conducted in-depth interviews three different time periods. The initial interview phase was conducted over a six-month interval from spring 2007 to winter 2008. The semi-

CHARACTERISTICS OF THE LABOR PROCESS IN INDEPENDENT PRODUCTIONS: The Digitalized Flexible Production Regime

The term "flexibility" is a hazy word at best. As Ursell (1998) summarized, however, a discussion of this concept can be divided into several aspects. In general, 'flexibility' is perceived as evidence of late capitalism as well as the fundamental transformation of capitalism (Ursell, 1998). The interpretation of such a change, however, differs between its supporters and critics. Its supporters (e.g., Piore and Sable, 1984) claim that the shift from large-scale, bureaucratic and corporate structures towards networks of interdependent and flexibly specialized small trades is a process of change that enhances the significant growth of economic and political democracy (Ursell, 1998: 129). By contrast, critics (e.g., Jessop, 1993), interpreting the significance of this change in other ways, perceive flexible production as a distinctive feature associated with the end of the Keynesian welfare state system. In other words, from the viewpoint of the critics, this shift reveals that "late capitalism in crisis restructures itself to maintain wage relations" (Ursell, 1998: 129).

One might argue that an alternative perspective on flexibility standpoints that focuses on the organizational level, such as that of a "flexible firm," is more useful here in analyzing the actual organizational characteristics of late capitalism. Atkinson's primitive yet still important core-periphery model suggests that the flexible firm—as an exemplar organizational structure of

structured questionnaire was constructed about labor conditions and processes as well as about recognition and coping with labor conditions. Participant observation was conducted in one IP company for two weeks in February 2008 in Yeoido where most IP companies are clustered and produce cultural and documentary programs. At that time, this company produced six programs for the networks and had 30 employees; the managers were former PDs of the networks. Based on the initial interview results, I reconducted interviews in 2017 in order to scrutinize whether the labor process and working conditions in the IP sector had changed over the ten-year period. The interviewees have more than 10 years work experiences in the sector, and they confirmed that there has not been much change in labor processes and working conditions. Rather, they reported that the trends that I found in my initial interviews actually have worsened over the past ten-year time span.

late capitalism—optimizes productivity by pursuing adaptable production that consists of the interrelationship of "numerical" and "functional" flexibility. Basically, he assumes that an organization's core is composed of those roles which are most vital to the firm and provide the basis of its key competence (Atkinson, 1987). In this situation, functional flexibility is concerned with "how the firm adjusts the deployment of these people and the contents of their jobs to meet the changing tasks generated by their workload" (Atkinson, 1987: 90). To accomplish these adjustments, he suggests that the firms seek to establish long-term relations with a group of highly committed and skilled employees. At the periphery, however, flexible firms "adjust the number of their workers or the number of hours they work, in line with changes in the level of demand for them" (Atkinson, 1989: 90). This simply means that the number of employees can be quickly and easily increased or decreased in line with even short-term changes at the level of the demand for labor. In short, the flexible firm is composed on the one hand of multi-skilled and stable core workers and on the other of contingent and insecure peripheral workers (the latter resulting from short-term hires, temporary help agencies, and contract companies) (Nesheim, Olsen, & Kalleberg, 2007).

Even though Atkinson does not mean that the flexible firm model is simply adopted as a capitalistic company's short-term cost-cutting strategy, he does point out that "the entire 'flexibility debate' has been conducted in terms of what flexibilities capital requires of labor" (Atkinson & Meager, 1986: 28). Ursell (1998) criticizes, however, that even if the flexible firm theory was not intended to be either prescriptive or political, it could not escape criticism. She notes that the flexible firm model, which assumes a principal form of managerially rational discrimination of the core from the periphery, can be said to support the development of a segmented or dual labor market (Ursell, 1998). Harrison (1994) also argues that the flexibility of large firms depends fundamentally on the perpetuation of contingent work, and that even a dual market can exist within single firms.

Kalleberge (2001) notes, moreover, that the flexible firm strategy involves the hiring of a sufficient number of employees to maximize productivity with minimal cost, but without the objective to protect even a core group of employees; this lack of protection is associated with pressures to minimize costs and motivated by the intention to reduce separation costs rather than to protect core employees. That is, even core workers do not tend to remain permanently with their employer, as their skills are portable. On the contrary, workers in the periphery have fewer alternatives to land comparable jobs in other organizations than do core workers, so employers often relegate these peripheral workers to the status of second-class workforces (Kalleberge, 2001: 493). Williamson (1975) also contends that within the shift towards a flexible market-oriented situation, the employees stand to lose not only income but also their rights, security, collegiality, identity and learning op-portunities. The employer, on the other hand, also stands to lose the em-ployees' trust, idiosyncratic knowledge of the work, loyalty, endeavor, com-mitment to product quality, and so on.

In summary, it can be seen that critics of the 'flexible firm' theory give careful attention to the results and effects of flexible production, regardless of the employers and employees. By considering these factors, I will delin-eate the actual labor conditions in the Korean IP sector by applying the core-periphery model, which is based on the interrelationship between two flexibility concepts: numerical and functional flexibility. By applying this model, I intend to clarify the characteristics of the labor process in Korean IP companies; in the next step, I will strive to find out the effects and results of flexible production on the workers in related to digitalization.

Numerical Flexibility

Given that there are no large-scale surveys of labor conditions within the Korean independent sector, this study focuses on uncovering experiences and meanings of "ordinary" or "typical" work experiences of the workers by using in-depth interviews and participant observation. My interview data show that freelance employment is the main practice of IP companies. Most of these contingent workers are hired at low salaries through oral contracts. Such informal contracts can lead to easy layoffs and place the employees at a disadvantage during disputes with employers. Obviously, this contingent work situation can be connected to the problem of low salaries. The salary gap between workers in the networks and the IP sector is wide. Interviewees reported that the average monthly payment for entry-level workers is approximately $500 to $1,000; for mid-level jobholders, $2,000 to $2,500; and for longtime workers, payment stagnated at $3,000 to $3,500. The most serious problem is that the minimum salary of starters who hold assistant positions, regardless of their jobs, is not enough even to cover basic living costs. Both of my recent interviewees whom I met in 2017 confirmed that the problem of low starting pay in the industry has not changed much at all in the last 10 to 15 years.

On the one hand, what is important is that economic distress, bad business, or oversupply of labor are not the only factors responsible for the low-pay practice for starters in the industry. On the other hand, there is societal discourse and cultural notions about broadcasting work that frames it not as "work" but rather as "art" based on long and hard apprenticeships, and such notions can propagate to retain this practice. One of my interviewees told me her own experience: when she started work at an IP company, her boss actually refused to pay her by arguing that she was not doing 'work;' rather he was actually giving her a 'training opportunity.' She revealed that this company owner said, "Why do I have to pay you? On the contrary, you have to pay me because I teach you."

Even though most workers retain their position under contingent contracts, their workloads are roughly the same or more than that of regular workers at the networks. Despite these intense workloads, however, they have fewer holidays than do other workers. Most of my interviewees answered that they cannot rest sufficiently in their line of work. They tend to work long hours, have fewer holidays and take fewer days off. In in-depth interviews, one lighting worker said his most difficult problem is not his salary, but the length of his working time. He usually comes to work at 5:00 a.m. and finishes at 2:00 a.m. the next day (21 hours later): he works for one day including overnight and then sleeps the next day. This does not leave him with much time to spend with his family. This kind of overnight working practice is found in other positions as well. One scriptwriter said that she usually works 12–14 hours a day, nearly seven days a week. She mentioned that her situation is common. A computer graphic worker said her schedule changes often and she also works too late. In this situation, it is difficult for her to make appointments with friends because of her irregular working hours.

In addition, unlike their counterparts in network broadcasting, many IP workers do not have employment insurance, national pensions, workmen accident compensation insurance, and health insurance. Moreover, they hardly enjoy the other forms of company support that the network workers receive, such as retirement grants, transportation allowances, and education allowances. The main reason why IP companies adopt this numerical flexibility strategy is their economic distress, based on the irregularity of program contracts and excessive competition among their type of company. One IP company owner said:

> We all know it is better to hire workers in regular positions to improve their skills, but it is too hard for us to employ most workers as regulars. Usually, we hire them after we get a program production contract with a network. Nevertheless, if the company loses its program production contract from the network due to the low program rating, we naturally have to break up the team. Otherwise, we would not be able to retain our business because we could not afford their labor cost. This is the usual business practice in this industry.

In summary, IP companies pursue numerical flexibility as a cost-cutting strategy, based on their business contexts. Nevertheless, the main problem appears to be the way that this increase in numerical flexibility causes insecurity and unstable working conditions for IP workers. This employment practice is simply adjusting to the economic situation under the pressure of budgetary circumstances. It thus can be said that the contemporary labor market in the Korean broadcasting industry is divided into two contrasting scenarios: while full-time workers in the major networks are hired with relatively high levels of income and job security, their IP counterparts are hired under conditions of relatively low income, excessive work hours, and unstable employment. These harsh working conditions are not caused solely by the practice of numerical flexibility. In the case of IP, the more important point is that the companies connect numerical flexibility with functional flexibility in their labor practices.

Digitalization and Functional Flexibility

One of the distinctive features of the emerging labor process in the IP sector can be seen as the relationship between digitalization and functional flexibility. The wide extent of the digital video technology is one of the critical factors rousing the change in the labor process within the independent sector. Interestingly, at the end of the 1990s a new group of workers emerged in the broadcasting industry who were called 'video journalists (VJs).' Many newspaper articles started to report on this new job and were pleased particularly with the appearance of VJs' television programming (e.g., Hankook Ilbo, 2001). According to these articles, the new job of the VJ began with Q Channel's documentary program in 1995 that had features which contained novel and innovative phrases (e.g., Hankook Ilbo, 2001). VJs are perceived as singlehandedly performing the entire program production process—from conception to editing—using a small, portable digital video camera (MiniDV) or high-end digital single-lens reflex (DSLR) camera to shoot along with a personal computer to edit. For this reason, the production process of VJs came to be called a "one-person production system," made possible by the introduction of digital technology; moreover, with regard to the content, VJs were inclined to find rarely selected TV content based on the MiniDV's portability. For example, the content of "VJ Tukgongdae," the nationally famous program produced by the VJ system, did not dwell on a celebrity but rather on the lives of ordinary people, shot with a fast-moving camera. After VJ programs became popular, they formed their own genre: the so-called "6mm program."

So-called "6mm programs" generally refer to cultural and documentary shows that are shot with a MiniDV or DSLR camera, which is cheaper than those shot with an ENG (Electronic News Gathering) camera. The program is typically recorded on various types of digital tapes, among them 6mm digital tape. Generally in the IP sector today, however, people refer to independent productions as '6mm programs,' which are mostly cultural and documentary programs that consist of many different short parts and brief production periods; moreover, they are shot with a MiniDV not by camerapeople but by program directors. From the viewpoint of network broadcasting, though, this production system is considered as both novel and of economic interest. When these '6mm programs' were introduced to the television industry, the networks were under budgetary pressure due to IMF intervention and the national economic crisis. These networks were able to reduce their production costs and financial risks by actively pursuing these types of programs which became popular to viewers due to their novelty while also pleasing the journalists (Moonhwa Ilbo, 1999).

Nonetheless, various problems and changes in the labor process associated with the emergence of these 6mm programs are becoming obvious and serious because this production practice—represented by short production time and cheap production costs—is becoming the typical production practice across the entire IP sector. Through the introduction of these 6mm programs, the networks have found a way to cut their production costs; likewise IP companies now also choose not to use cameramen and a lighting crew to reduce their production costs. The problem is that it is becoming unavoidable for IP companies to produce only such 6mm programs to survive in the industry. One scriptwriter revealed that IP companies used to produce more varied programs before the emergence of the 6mm format. The reason why IPs make only '6mm programs' is to save on production costs. More importantly, this interviewee points out that this trend is based not only on IP companies' own interests; rather the network broadcasters also prefer '6mm programs' from these independent contractors due to the cost savings. She reported that the usual production cost of 6mm programs is about 15,000 US dollars, but if a program uses an ENG camera the cost usually doubles. So she observed that it is almost impossible for IP companies to survive unless they produce 6mm programs. There appears to be valuable advantages with the use of the MiniDV for some types of shows because of its mobility and timeliness. The problem, however, is that the use of a MiniDV is based not on the character of a program but rather on economic factors, thus being used inappropriately for shows that require clearer images and slower scene transitions. One IP company owner talked plainly about this issue:

> The networks also know that independent productions extensively use MiniDVs. I don't think the technology itself is notorious because it has its own features. This camera really suits productions that require portability and promptness. Yet the problem is that most independent producers today have no choice but to produce programs using only this small camera, unlike the networks. Everybody knows that image quality deteriorates with this camera, and the change of scene is too fast. For me, this situation is quite serious.

Thus one of the more notable changes is that the increase in the number of these '6mm programs' is actually leading to changes in the labor process within the independent sector. First, it is bringing about a change of roles among various jobs. For example, from the use of MiniDVs the role of the producer and the cameraperson is merged into one job; consequentially my interviewees protest that in order to decrease their production costs, producers prefer to use the MiniDV which they can run by themselves rather than use an ENG camera which needs the professional control of a cameraperson. One interviewee reported that due to the wide use of MiniDVs, many ENG camerapeople are out of work now. He said that while many of his co-workers have quit this job, he also worried that the more serious problem lies with the decline in the quality of images (pictures) that non-experts have taken. Most of my interviewees agree that it is getting difficult to find camerapeople in the independent sector.

Secondly, with such changes in roles, the increase in the functional flexibility of the producer is causing a role reversion between producers and scriptwriters. A producer habitually takes the leadership role in the production process in the Korean broadcasting industry, but the leadership of the scriptwriter tends to increase in the production process with the creation of '6mm programs' in the independent sector. The main reason for such a role reversion is the transition of job responsibilities of the producer from 'planning and conceptualizing' to 'shooting and editing.' One scriptwriter said that usually the role of scriptwriters is greater in a 6mm program production: they conceptualize, arrange the programs, and even liaison with interviewees while producers, according to their guidelines, tend to focus on such technical work as shooting. Such leadership transitions are influencing the labor process negatively. One scriptwriter criticizes this situation:

> Nowadays, producers in IP companies are no more than cameramen. As their [PD] position is downgraded, the writer's role is emphasized as a leading creator in planning and making programs. Even independent PDs don't have enough time to think about the program because they are too busy going on location or editing. Also, to meet the industry demand, young assistants are becoming producers too fast despite their immaturity (because it is easy to learn to shoot a film with a MiniDV). These situations are giving writers important roles, and it is becoming more likely for us to become exhausted mentally.

As shown in the above interview, in IP companies producers have to take on the role of camerapeople while scriptwriters have to share the role of producers. For this reason, scriptwriters feel more pressure than previously because of the increase in their workload. Likewise, producers also feel more pressure because they have to shoot and edit by themselves. This technical multi-tasking deprives them of the time to think and plan programs and strips away at their identity as producers. When I asked producers about the relationship between 6mm programs and their role, they avoided answering and objected when I suggested to them that the scriptwriter's role is getting larger. They said they also hope ultimately to produce ENG programs, given more abundant financial support and longer production time. In fact, almost everyone agreed that their multiple roles now are based not on their own choice but rather on budgetary pressures.

A third serious change that has emanated from the increase in the number of 6mm programs is the increasing emergence of non-skilled workers. As occupational roles change, the chronic and rigid apprentice system that has existed for a long time in the Korean broadcasting labor process is also gradually declining. In each occupation, senior workers instructed assistants over a long period of time until their ability was developed enough and proven. In the current IP sector, however, apprenticeships are declining due to cost savings pursuits and increased workloads. One assistant producer and scriptwriter commented about these changes in apprenticeship:

> I (assistant producer) think we have to receive more training from senior producers to improve our skills. In reality, however, we are too busy to learn and our seniors are too busy to train us. The production time is too short and the workload is too much. Despite our lack of systematic training, however, we ADs become producers right away if we can use a MiniDV. In the networks, assistant producers are trained step by step for five years to become producers. This difference in training leads to an incompetence of producers.

> In networks, ADs are usually trained for four or five years to become producers. In independent production companies, however, ADs usually become PDs after two years or even one year if they can shoot well (using a MiniDV). That's why we (scriptwriters) have to guide and lead them. Actually, I have learned a lot of things [from] inside PDs, but nothing [from] outside PDs. . . . They are quite different.

As shown in the above interviews, many workers agreed that the time period for becoming a producer is getting shorter while opportunities for skills acquisition are becoming fewer. Moreover, the proliferation of 6mm programs is one reason behind the role reversal between producers and scriptwriters. Also, the decrease in apprenticeships is noted among other jobs as well. One cameraperson reported that because of the decrease in demand, a full-time assistant cameraperson is no longer necessary in the IP sector. Now, he can get a temporary assistant from a job agency occasionally to meet demand; consequentially, he treats these temporary assistants not as trainees but as solely one-day helpers. At the same time, as apprenticeships in the IP sector are disappearing, the number of job agencies is increasing. With such an increase in broadcasting employment agencies, temporary workers joining the agencies cannot build their career and skills consistently. Therefore, the collapse of apprenticeships without an alternative training system is causing an increase in the number of non-skilled workers. Ultimately, this lack of training can be linked to the deterioration of program quality.

Finally, the changing labor process in the independent sector contributes to limiting the pursuit of creativity. Most workers feel their creativity is limited under this harsh working situation. The producer directs more energy towards technical aspects while the scriptwriter feels more mental fatigue due to the increase in workload. Moreover, technical workers also blame the excessively short production intervals for 6mm programs. One audio director commented on the increasing demand for speed in cultural programs. Due to the time pressure in producing programs, it is hard to display his creativity; therefore in this limited working situation, independents are becoming more 'workers,' as he put it, than 'creators.'

The increase in functional flexibility becomes available due to technological innovations, but the main reason for such an increase is based on the economic situation of IP companies. Furthermore, this tendency toward an increase in functional flexibility in turn is changing many aspects of the labor process within the independent sector. To sum up, four distinctive situations occur in the labor process within the independent sector. Firstly, the roles of workers are changing into new staff divisions, such as with the decrease in the number of camerapeople and lighting staff needed. Secondly, leadership in the program production process is gradually shifting from the producer to the scriptwriter with both roles feeling much pressure because of the burden of increasing workloads. Thirdly, under these changes, it is easy to predict that the tendency towards a non-skilled labor process will occur in most jobs within the independent sector. In particular, the decline in traditional apprenticeships without practical alternatives is worsening the situation. Fourthly with these changes, it is reasonable for IP workers to recognize their limitations in pursuing creativity.

CONCLUDING REMARKS

From the viewpoint of Atkinson's core-periphery model, the core and the periphery can be distinguished by the character of a job. He defines 'core workers' as "those whom firms regard as their most important and most unique workers" (Atkinson, 1987: 93). In contrast, he defines 'peripheral workers' as those who perform "what the firm regards as its routine and mechanical activities." Core workers are perceived as those who cannot be readily recruited outside while periphery workers are opposite to core workers (Atkinson, 1987: 93). With this framework, it is possible to apply the core-peripheral model to the organizational structure of the Korean Broadcasting Industry.

At the organizational level, the core worker of a television production organization, particularly in the networks, traditionally has been the head of a production unit, namely, the producer; this role has evolved because the quality of a creative job has become regarded as the very foundation of the competitive power of broadcasting. The external production policy that aims to externalize a production unit from the networks, however, can mean that production jobs, such as those of producers who are at the traditional core, are starting no longer to be perceived as central. As long as the major networks generally criticize the policy and retain their internal labor market, they will continue to regard production roles, especially that of a producer, as core jobs. At this point, the underlying notions and situation of workers at the networks versus at IP companies are showing different trends. As shown above, the IP companies are simultaneously pursuing numerical and functional flexibility even among such core workers as producers and scriptwriters.

At this point, it can be seen that the same production job can be differentially treated in accordance with which type of organization (networks vs. independent) one works.

Accordingly, Nesheim and his colleagues (2007) report that the trend of non-standard employment relations in ICT industries differs according to the character of an organization. In particular, organizations with innovation strategies are more likely to use consulting firms in their core activities, while organizations that compete on the basis of low cost are more apt to use temporary help agencies. From this viewpoint, while the workers introduced by consulting firms have functional flexibility, the workers from temporary help agencies by contrast specialize in numerical flexibility. That is, companies using low-cost strategies tend to pursue numerical flexibility even in their core groups. At this point, IP companies are showing typical features of cost-oriented firms by pursuing numerical flexibility among their core workers such as producers and scriptwriters.

Moreover, the more important point is the character of functional flexibility, which the IP companies are fulfilling. It cannot be easily said that the convergence trend is regarded as negative in its totality. As stated above, the newly emerging producer model, VJ, is contributing to the creation of a new genre which is overcoming the limited production environment via novelty and mobility, but the excessive and monotonous production process that focuses only on producing 6mm programs is triggering and exacerbating the emergence of unskilled workers and excessive workloads. Nesheim and his colleagues (2007) claim that core workers can be divided into on the one hand "qualitative workers" who include "specially competent workers" accomplished in innovation-oriented firms, and on the other "numerical workers" who display an "extra capacity" in cost-oriented firms. Following this distinction, it may be argued that the functional flexibility pursued by IP companies improves only the extra capacity of the producer (e.g., more technical multitasking that includes shooting and editing) that is usually executed in organizations with low-cost strategies. In short, it is important to note that the labor process in IP companies is undergoing changes towards the convergence of various jobs, not with the explicit aim to improve the competence and expertise of workers but rather to cut production costs as a means of business survival.

Youn and Jang (2002) insist that the value of broadcasting programs should not be determined by the efficacy of their production nor the maximization of profit, but by the quality of the program and its cultural, social and public contributions. In this regard, these scholars suggest that vital labor power, which can provide various and high-quality ideas to the public, be derived from stable training, experience, and education. In keeping with its vision, the present labor process in the Korean independent sector— which connects numerical to functional flexibility and is regulated and fitted not by promoting the quality of expertise but by the company's cost-cutting —is a burden and barrier to the development and enhancement of both the quality of its programs as well as its workers' creativity. From the viewpoint of IP companies, technological innovation ignited by the usage of digital technology allows them to reduce their production costs and produce the new, so-called "6mm program" genre so that the production system in the IP sector can become flexible and innovative. However, the digitalization of this production process paradoxically limits its workers' capability to improve and enhance their skills and creativity. In this regard, we should ask: can the present system be a sustainable reproduction system not only from the viewpoint of the industry, but also of its workers as well?

References

Atkinson, J. (1987). Flexibility or fragmentation? the United Kingdom labour market in the eighties. *Labour and Society*, 12(1): 87–105.

Atkinson, J. & Meager, N. (1986). Is Flexible Just a Flash in the Pan?, *Personnel Management*, September: 26–29.

Christopherson, S. (2008). Beyond the self-expressive creative worker: an industry perspective on entertainment media. *Theory, Culture and Society*, 25(7–8): 73–95.

Chosun Ilbo. (2010). China should learn Korea's cultural content exportation strategy. [cited 5 April 2010]. Available from http://newsplus.chosun.com/site/data/html_dir/2010/04/05/2010040501504.html

Day, W. (2007). Commodification of creativity: reskilling computer animation labor in Taiwan. In V. Mosco & C. McKerche (eds.). *Knowledge Workers in the Information Society* (pp. 85–100). Lanhan: Lexington Books.

Evans, P. (1995). *Embedded autonomy: states and industrial transformation*. Princeton, NJ: Princeton University Press.

Hankook Ilbo (2001). Rising VJ as a Guerrilla of Broadcasting [Cited 11 March 2001].

Hankook KyungJae (2010). Ministry of Culture will invest billion dollars in cultural industry. [Cited 22 November 2010]. Available from: http://www.hankyung.com/news/app/newsview.php?aid=2010112224248&intype=1

Harrison, B. (1994). *Lean and Mean: The Changing Landscape of Corporate Power in the Age of Flexibility*. New York: Basic Books.

Hesmondhalgh, D. & Baker, S. (2008). Creative work and emotional labour in the television industry. *Theory, Culture and Society*, 25(7–8): 97–118.

Huat, C. B. & Iwabuchi, K. (2008). *East Asian pop culture: analyzing the Korean wave*. Hong Kong: Hong Kong University Press.

Jessop, B. (1993). Toward a Schumpeterian Workfare State? Preliminary Remarks on Post-Fordist Political Economy, *Studies in Political Economy*, 40: 7–39

Jin, D. (2007). Reinterpretation of cultural imperialism: emerging domestic market vs continuing US dominance. *Media, Culture and Society*, 29(5): 753–771.

KBI (2002). *Digitalsidae bangsongilluk sukup jungchaek* [*Study on the broadcasting human resource policy in digital era*]. Seoul: Commbooks.

_____ (2004). *Bangssongsanup bijungujik siltaewa gaesun banghyange kwanhan yunku* [*Study on labor condition of contingent work on Korean broadcasting industry*]. Seoul: Commbooks.

Kim, H. M. (2005). The cultural industry and gendered labor: with an emphasis on women writers in the television program broadcast industry. *Journal of Korean Women's Studies*, 21(2): 69–103.

Kallerberg, A. (2001). Organizing Flexibility: the Flexible Firm in a New Century, *British Journal of Industrial Relations*, 39(4): 479–504.

KOBACO (2005). *Doklipjejaksa siltae josayungu* [*Study on the actual conditions of Korean independent broadcasting production company*]. Seoul: KOBACO.

Lee, K. (2009). A final flowering of the developmental state: the IT policy experiment of the Korean Information Infrastructure 1995–2005. *Government Information Quarterly*, 26: 567–576.

McRobbie, A. (2016). *Be creative.* London: Polity.

Miller, T., Govil, N., McMurria, J., Maxwell, R., & Wang, T. (2005). *Global Hollywood 2.* London: BFI Publishing.

Moonhwa Ilbo (1999). Do You Know Video Journalist? [Cited 30 July, 1999].

Mosco, V. & Steven, A. (2007). Outsourcing knowledge work: labor responds to the new international division of labor. In V. Mosco & C. McKerche (eds.). *Knowledge Workers in the Information Society* (pp. 147–162). Lanhan: Lexington Books.

Nesheim, T., Olsen, K., & Kalleberg, A. (2007). Externalizing the Core: Firms' Use of Employment Intermediaries in the Information and Communication Technology Industries, *Human Resource Management*, 46(2): 247–264.

Piore, M. & Sable, C. (1984). *The Second Industrial Divide*, New York: Basic Books.

Qiu, J. & Kim, Y. (2010). Recession and progression? notes on media, labor, and youth from East Asia. *International Journal of Communication*, 4: 630–648.

Ryoo, W. (2008). The political economy of the global mediascape: the case of the South Korean film industry. *Media, Culture and Society*, 30(8): 873–889.

Shim, D. (2006). The growth of Korea cultural industries and the Korean wave. In K. Chan & I. Koichi (eds.). *East Asian Pop Culture: Analyzing the Korean Wave* (pp. 175–189), Hong Kong: Hong Kong University Press.

Sullivan, J. (2007). Marketing creative labor: Hollywood 'making of' documentary features In V. Mosco & C. McKerche (eds.). *Knowledge Workers in the Information Society* (pp. 69–84). Lanhan: Lexington Books.

Ursell, G. (1998). Labour Flexibility in the UK Commercial Television Sector, *Media, culture & society*, 20(1): 129–153.

_____ (2000). Television production: issues of exploitation, commodification and subjectivity. *Media, Culture and Society*, 22(6): 805–825.

Williamson, O. (1975). *Market and Hierarchies: Analysis and Antitrust Implications.* New York: The Free Press.

Yeo, J. (2006). *The TV Broadcasting Industry and Regulations in China.* Seoul: KIEP.

Youn, S., & Jang, H. (2002). The policy of programming quota increase of the independent production sector in the over-the-air TV programming in South Korea. *Korean Journal of Broadcasting*, 16(2): 242–274.

digital
KOREA

Digital Technology and People's Lives

How the Digital Technology and Environment Changed People's Lives in The Advertising Industry

8

Taemin Kim

Incheon National University

In recent years, technological advances have both shaped the future of advertising and led the many changes within the industry (Kumar and Gupta, 2018). Technology has made target segmentation more precise and real-time responses of advertisers possible (Nesamoney, 2015). Specifically, the digital environment represented by the Internet and social media have been changing the traditional forms of advertising (Okazaki and Taylor, 2013). The Internet and social media made two-way communications between advertisers and consumers both easy and convenient, and the ability to interact and engage with consumers has become important to advertisers (Wu, 2016). Additionally, as a consequence of these changes, consumers have become more empowered (Powers et al., 2012). No longer are consumers simple message recipients but active evaluators who can provide feedback directly to the companies (i.e., advertisers). Furthermore, they can share their opinions about the ads and advertised products with other consumers. Korea is no exception to these changes in advertising. In Korea, digital advertising is expected to account for 33% of total advertising spending in 2017. Although TV advertising spending constitutes 36.1% of total advertising spending, it grew by a mere .9%, whereas digital advertising grew by 8.9% compared with the previous year (KAA, 2016). In 2018, digital advertising spending is expected to exceed TV advertising spending. Additionally, Korea's telecommunication and Internet infrastructure have been among the top advanced levels, thus the adoption of new technology in the Korean advertising industry is likely to be more prevalent than other markets (Shin, 2014).

These changes in advertising caused by technological advances are bringing challenges to advertisers because the previously existing media and target audiences have become fragmented and thus much harder to reach than before (Powers et al., 2016). At the same time, these changes can serve as great opportunities for businesses wishing to reach both existing and new customers. The Internet and social media enable advertisers to segment the target market and audiences more precisely, and to customize the messages and media vehicles that deliver the advertisements (Kumar and Gupta, 2016). Considering both the challenges and opportunities, it is no wonder there the attention paid to these changes in advertising under the recent digital environment has been on the steep upswing (Kerr et al., 2015).

However, most studies on the changes in the digital environment have focused on what new advertising service will be introduced and what new technology will be applied to the advertising industry without a theoretical background (Kumar and Gupta, 2016). Few studies have focused on the people who work in the advertising industry under the ever-changing digital environment. Specifically, little research has been conducted focusing on changes in the employees' work and their lives in the Korean advertising industry. Thus, the purpose of this study is to explore how the digital environment has changed employees' work in the Korean advertising industry, and how those changes have shaped those people's lives in Korea. Furthermore, this study investigated these topics based on a theoretical framework adapted from a sociotechnical systems approach.

LITERATURE REVIEW

Social and Technological Perspectives: A Sociotechnical Systems Approach

A sociotechnical systems approach proposes that a technological perspective should be considered along with a social perspective to investigate the changes in work and work processes caused by new technology (Appelbaum, 1997). In other words, technological and social perspectives are not separate and are interrelated. Applying this approach to people working in organizations and work processes, it suggests that the interaction between technology and employees in workplaces is important to explain organizational development and changes in their work or work processes. This interaction between the infrastructure and humans is also important to understand the complex phenomena in workplaces caused by technological advances (Zammuto and O'Connor, 1992; Berg, 1999). The current study adopts this sociotechnical systems (STS) approach to explore changes in advertising work and to investigate the implications for people whose lives might be impacted by those changes.

Applying this approach, it becomes evident that new technology is causing changes in advertising work and work processes, and this will influence the lives of people working in the advertising industry. This gives rise the question: How does new technology and the digital environment affect employees' work in the advertising industry? First, employees working in the advertising industry should become conscious of consumers' opinions on the Internet and be ready to quickly respond to them. Consumers can post their feedback any time on Facebook or Twitter, and they soon become accustomed to receiving responses and answers from the companies in real time (Campbell et al., 2011). The digital environment and digital advertising enable consumers to interact with companies (advertisers) through social media or on the Internet. Thus, advertisers, recognizing the necessity, continually monitor consumers' responses and respond to them quickly.

Second, the digital environment and new technology enable advertisers to create and implement more targeted and relevant advertising campaigns. On

Facebook, advertisers can choose specific characteristics of target audiences such as gender, locations, interests, ages, and so on (Facebook, 2018). Furthermore, the recent advent of big data technology allows the implementation of advertising campaigns to more specifically targeted consumers and the analysis of their behaviors (Kumar et al., 2013). The digital environment also enables advertisers to produce more contextually relevant advertising messages (Kumar and Gupta, 2016). For example, if a person shows an interest in a product by searching for a specific product on the Internet, he or she would see the ad of the product and relevant advertising message later. It is called a personalized ad, and it helps him or her to search for more information about the product or a make a purchase decision on that product (Tucker, 2014).

On the contrary, new technology does not affect people's work and their lives unilaterally. Based on the STS approach, social structure, culture, and people's behavior would affect how advertisers use technology for their advertising campaigns. These days, consumers actively deliver their opinions about an ad and its product directly to the company (Azar et al., 2016). After watching a new ad on YouTube, consumers can leave comments on that venue. They can share their opinions with other friends on Facebook and Twitter. Advertisers often want to figure out consumers' opinions about their new product and commercials. Previously, they needed to conduct a consumer survey called a post copy test to grasp consumers' responses on the aired commercial. Now it is easier to receive consumers' honest feedback and it is almost cost-free because advertisers can grasp consumers' opinions through social media easily and at little expense. Those consumers' opinions are considered critical in the digital age. For example, Pepsi launched a new commercial in 2017, whose message was about encouraging youth activism and fighting for social equality. However, the ad was seriously criticized by consumers, and Pepsi decided to pull the ad (Schultz and Diaz, 2017). Thus, advertisers often create ads that are intended to engage consumers more actively. In other words, social and cultural changes have transformed how technology can best be used in the industry. Advertisers often develop ads with the intention of soliciting consumers' feedback (Kumar and Gupta,

2016; Magno, Cassia, and Bruni, 2017). Furthermore, some advertisers encourage consumers to participate in their marketing communications and content production, which is called co-created contents (Constantinides, Brünink, and Lorenzo-Romero, 2015). To do so, advertisers need to utilize new technology proficiently and prepare themselves for collecting and analyzing consumer feedback in real time (Lohr, 2012). That is why many companies are interested in big data technology and new technology in advertising (Kumar and Gupta, 2016). These changes in the advertising industry can be interpreted in terms of a social and cultural change. In the web 2.0 era, interactivity and engagement with consumers is one of the most important missions for companies that conduct marketing and advertising (Campbell et al., 2011).

Thus, social and cultural changes in the industry are bringing about changes in how to use technology and how it is applied to the industry. To actively interact with consumers, advertisers seek to operate and manage multiple channels on the Internet and social media.

In addition to these changes at the industry and social levels, a change at an individual level frequently leads to changes in advertising work and employees' lives. Han (2015) suggested that we live in the era of fatigue and in the "burnout society." He argued that people in the burnout society often exploit themselves and do so voluntarily to succeed in the future. Employees are becoming more exhausted, but they think (or want to believe) they are happy and willing to work more instead of complaining and resisting negative environments in their work and personal lives. Interestingly, people in the burnout society are armed with positive and optimistic perspectives on their lives despite extreme competition and stress. It is a different phenomenon from past generations who also worked hard and often exploited themselves, but they did so involuntarily due to compulsion and under the orders of their superiors. In the burnout society, technological advances reinforce this trend. Technology enables employees to continue to work outside the office without overtime pay even when resting at home after their work hours. The difference between the burnout society and the previous society is people are more than willing to work overtime and feel secure while exploiting themselves (Han, 2015).

Put together, the interrelationship between technology, social/cultural changes, and individuals' behavioral changes, provides the implications of how the digital environment has changed employees' work and their lives in the advertising industry. The next chapter discusses these issues by using an interview methodology with employees working in the advertising industry.

METHOD

To investigate how people working in the advertising industry think about the changes and challenges in their field of work, a qualitative research approach was adopted to this study. Specifically, an in-depth interview methodology was used. To do so, snowball sampling was used to identify and recruit employees working in the advertising industry. All respondents have worked in the advertising industry for at least 13 years, specifically in the digital advertising field. Previously, they had experienced working in the traditional advertising field focusing on TV and print media advertising. Some of them work in both fields now. The average number of years working in the advertising industry is 14.3 years. Additionally, to investigate the perspectives of both an advertiser and an advertising agency, this study recruited employees from the client side (i.e., an advertiser or company that plans and sponsors an ad) and the advertising agency side (i.e., an advertising agency that has developed an actual advertising campaign). During January and February 2018, three interviews were conducted, which were recorded by using a smartphone (a voice-recording application in iPhone 5s). The interviews ran between 50 and 80 minutes (see Appendices A and B for the interview questions and descriptions of the respondents). The number of respondents is three, aged 40 to 45, one of whom is male.

RESULTS

Much to Be Done: Quantitatively and Qualitatively Overworking

In the digital and social media era, the media and audiences are becoming fragmented (Truong, McColl, and Kitchen, 2010). For example, previously, when implementing an advertising campaign, the primary media consisted of television, radio, and newspaper. These days, there are multiple social networking services to advertise brands, such as Facebook, Instagram, Twitter, and do on. On the Internet, there are numerous websites where advertisements can be implemented. Thus, advertisers find themselves having to deal with multiple media and devices, such as mobile phones and tablets, to implement and manage their advertising campaigns (Kumar and Gupta, 2016). This leads to excessive work required of the employees. In sponsorship marketing, things are more complicated. For example, if a company wants to sponsor a sport event, they frequently should establish contract with multiple media outlets, such as a network TV station, a cable TV station, a portal website (e.g., *Naver* in Korea), and a newspaper company:

> A: There has become a lot of work to do these days in the digital age. There are multiple media and devices such as mobile phones that we should handle and manage. . . . Previously, we sponsored a star soccer player to promote our brand on the Internet, so we planned to create a dedicated channel within an Internet portal service. We wanted to promote our brand through the popular soccer player. It appeared simple, but there were a lot of issues and challenges to implement the sponsorship campaign. First, the Internet portal service company had to create digital contents by using the player and our brand. To do so, a lot of specific digital contents had to be created, which means advertisers should review all of them and make a lot of decisions before implementing them. Another issue is users can copy the digital contents and share them with other users. Some users post positive comments and evaluations on the contents, but others share negative comments on

them or spoof the contents and share them with others. But we cannot control those negative reviews and contents. Another issue is the management's lack of understanding of digital media and digital contents. They always emphasize the importance of digital media and social media, but they usually pay more attention to traditional media such as TV and newspapers. They are not good at handling digital media, and sometimes they do not have an account on Facebook. It seems the management becomes more satisfied when our brand and product is exposed in TV news and in newspapers that they are more familiar with than when it is in digital media or social media. Despite that, they always emphasize that digital media is the number one priority in our communication and advertising.

The digital environment also qualitatively increases employees' work. As noted earlier, the digital environment and social media enable consumers to be more empowered. Consumers can give feedback to advertisers on their advertising campaigns in social media and try to share their opinions about the campaigns and brands with other consumers (Labrecque, 2013). Furthermore, mobile devices such as a smartphone enable consumers to show and share their opinions anywhere anytime (Grewal et al., 2016). These changes can have positive effects on advertisers' marketing campaigns by helping advertisers and advertising agencies develop more creative, interactive, and engaging campaigns (Kumar and Gupta, 2016). At the same time, they might have negative effects on employees working in the advertising industry. Employees such as marketers and advertising people in companies (advertisers) and advertising agencies frequently need to monitor consumer feedback even after normal work hours. This means they are often compelled to work extra hours at home without overwork pay:

B: My boss often sends a text message at night to ask a question or ask for an update on a recently launched campaign or a particular issue of our campaign or company. Whenever receiving the text, I get very stressed out and nervous. Even to answer a simple question, I do multiple searches, studies, and make several phone calls at night. I don't think the issue that my boss raised was urgent. It might be okay to handle and report it tomorrow. Sometimes, my boss sends a text message in a group chat room by using KakaoTalk (a mobile instant messaging application that is widely used in Korea for smartphones). So, I and our colleagues get more nervous and stressed when receiving it in the group chatting room because the boss can see who the first respondent is. It feels like we are competing with each other to answer the question more quickly and more thoroughly. But most issues turned out not to be an urgent and very critical issue.

Furthermore, employees working in the advertising industry need to be more vigilant when working, even after normal work hours, because they cannot guess what consumer feedback they will receive, when they will receive it, and how critical it might be. Some consumers' opinions should be dealt with quickly and seriously. Thus, they tend to keep monitoring consumer feedback in social media and comment sections on news websites. Some respondents said that they kept checking the News Feed posts on Facebook and consumer comment sections on YouTube continuously. Some employees reported that they were obsessed with checking them:

A: I keep watching the major portal websites on the Internet and social networking service sites to check consumer feedback on our campaigns and rival companies' communications. I try to identify common topics and ideas in consumer feedback. My boss puts pressure on me to keep monitoring and tracking consumer feedback. Combining the boss's pressure with the easy-to-use and fast digital technology, I have no choice but to keep working, checking, and updating.

A Vague Boundary between Working and Leisure Time

Given that employees are under pressure to overwork and are continuously monitored, employees tend to work even in their leisure time. With their smartphones, employees can keep checking consumer feedback on their advertising campaigns and the brands. They often collect and summarize such examples of feedback to report them to the management in real time. The management needs to know consumers' responses and the effectiveness of the advertising campaign in real time. The management believes it is easy for the employees to do so quickly. Employees often receive text messages after work hours through a smartphone messenger program:

> A: When I take a rest at home or even have dinner at a restaurant, I always keep my smartphone handy and keep checking for consumer feedback and a text message from the management and my boss. If I cannot answer the text message quickly, I feel very guilty and some-times my boss complains about my slow response.

The demand for real-time consumer feedback and reports on rival compa-nies' activities from the management or boss was often indirectly made to employees. The management would not clearly tell employees to work after normal work hours. Instead, they often ask a simple question or ask them to check the status of the campaigns. However, even a simple question and slight interest in competitors can act as a large pressure on employees. To satisfy the management's need, employees tend to sacrifice their leisure time and keep reporting to them until the management is satisfied. This might disrupt a work-life balance that has been considered critical for happiness up to now.

> B: My boss usually uses KakaoTalk to ask a question of me. He tells me and other colleagues to do something after work hours. He does not say if it is urgent or not. Sometimes I have no idea of whether it should be taken care of right now or tomorrow in my working hours. But I cannot ask about how urgent it is because I am worried my boss is not comfortable. I am often stressed because the issue does not appear ur-gent, but it feels like I have to do it right now. If I cannot do it quickly, it might make me lazy and not good at handling digital technology.

Pressure for Up-to-Date Information

In the traditional advertising era, no radical changes took place in advertising work and media environments. However, in the digital and social media era, there have been numerous changes in advertising work every day, specifically the changes caused by new technology. For example, 360-degree virtual reality video advertising was invented recently. This technology was quite new, so not all advertisers know about it, or have used it before. However, if a rival company uses this technology first for its new campaign, employees who do not use it yet could be reprimanded for failing to figure out the competitor's use of the new technology. Thus, employees would feel pressure to learn any up-to date information about new technology and competitors' activities.

> C: I always feel pressured to have a broad knowledge of new technology and applications to advertising. So, I habitually search for information on the Internet and read many trade magazines, even foreign magazines such as *Advertising Age*. I also search for news articles and blog articles from experts and ordinary people. If I find something useful, I read and save them for later. But sometimes I just surf the Internet without a clear objective, and I just do it to save useful information that I will never read later. If I stop doing it, I feel very guilty and I think I will fall behind. So, I cannot stop searching for new and updated information.

DISCUSSION

This study investigated how the digital environment has changed employees' work and their work processes, and how those changes have shaped people's personal lives in the Korean advertising industry. Employees working in the Korean advertising industry tend to overwork more than they did under the conditions of traditional advertising work and, increasingly, are under pressure to monitor consumers' feedback and competitors' activities in real time. They sometimes sacrifice their leisure time to do this, which can disrupt the balance between work and life. The management's indirect order or expectation often makes this situation worse. Furthermore, the management puts pressure on employees to be prepared for new technology and be armed with up-to date information and aware of new trends in the industry. The reasons for these changes in their work and work processes are complicated. Firstly, the primary reason is the recent surge of technological innovation. The digital environment and social media have enabled consumers to be more empowered and advertisers to manage their advertising campaigns in real time. Advertisers can change their strategies and tactics in real time based on consumer feedback and the management's request even though the campaigns were already launched (Nichols, 2013).

Secondly, these technological advances have changed the management's perspective toward advertising work and their employees' work. The management knows how technology has changed traditional advertising and how advertising has evolved. However, they do not completely understand the changes in advertising work processes. They simply ask employees to monitor consumer feedback and report rival companies' campaigns more often. This leads employees to work overtime voluntarily and stay vigilant after work. It also results in an unclear boundary between the working time and leisure time of employees, which could disrupt the balance between work and personal life.

Thirdly, along with technological and social pressure for changes, individuals as employees working in the advertising industry voluntarily participate in working overtime. It could not be precisely explained by a sociotechnical system approach because it is based on individual and voluntary behavior. As Han (2015) suggested, in the burnout society, people tend to work overtime voluntarily, and they are not satisfied with their accomplishments and their completed work. They feel compelled to keep working more and more to succeed. The issue is they do not complain and do not think they are unhappy. While they try to exploit themselves, they have positive and optimistic perspectives on their future, work, and lives. It might be natural to them to work much more and harder without overtime pay to survive in a highly competitive society. In a sense, they might take it for granted to be connected digitally 24 hours a day and 7 days a week, and they even think it is cool to work and live seamlessly connected to the network.

Lastly, a common negative feeling in the three interviews is guilt. If they do not respond to the boss's text message quickly, they feel guilty. Even though they cannot work hard after normal working hours, they usually feel that way. Feeling guilty would also be associated with their efforts to search for information and get consumer feedback on the Internet and social media. As one respondent mentioned, the Internet and social media technology induce them to search endlessly for new information and continuously work at any time anywhere. Although they do not need to work during their leisure time, they sometimes feel guilty because they seem to be worried about falling behind in the competition.

In addition to technological and social perspectives in people's live in the digital age, this study mentions the personal and individual perspectives on the changes in their work and lives by adopting the concept of the burnout society coined by Han (2015). However, there should be more investigation at the personal and individual level and changes caused by individual influence in the future. Additionally, given that advertising work processes are different based on company size, comparing employees' work and lives in a small-scale company with those in a large-scale company might be meaningful for the future study.

References

Appelbaum, S. H. (1997). Socio-technical systems theory: an intervention strategy for organizational development. *Management Decision*, 35(6): 452–463.

Azar, S. L., Machado, J. C., Vacas-de-Carvalho, L., & Mendes, A. (2016). Motivations to interact with brands on Facebook-Towards a typology of consumer-brand interactions. *Journal of Brand Management*, 23(2): 153–178.

Berg, M. (1999). Patient care information systems and health care work: a sociotechnical approach. *International Journal of Medical Informatics*, 55(2): 87–101.

Campbell, C., Pitt, L. F., Parent, M., & Berthon, P. R. (2011). Understanding consumer conversations around ads in a Web 2.0 world. *Journal of Advertising*, 40(1): 87–102.

Constantinides, E., Brünink, L. A., & Lorenzo-Romero, C. (2015). Customer motives and benefits for participating in online co-creation activities. *International Journal of Internet Marketing and Advertising*, 9(1): 21–48.

Facebook (2018), Ad Format Specs & Recommendations. Retrieved January 26, 2018, from https://www.facebook.com/business/ads-guide

Grewal, D., Bart, Y., Spann, M., & Zubcsek, P. P. (2016). Mobile advertising: a framework and research agenda. *Journal of Interactive Marketing*, 34: 3–14.

Han, B. C. (2015). *The Burnout Society*. Stanford, California: Stanford Briefs, an imprint of Stanford University Press.

Kerr, G., Schultz, D. E., Kitchen, P. J., Mulhern, F. J., & Beede, P. (2015). Does traditional advertising theory apply to the digital world?: a replication analysis questions the relevance of the elaboration likelihood model. *Journal of Advertising Research*, 55(4): 390–400.

Kumar, V., Bhaskaran, V., Mirchandani, R., & Shah, M. (2013). Practice prize winner— creating a measurable social media marketing strategy: increasing the value and ROI of intangibles and tangibles for hokey pokey. *Marketing Science*, 32(2): 194–212.

Labrecque, L. I., vor dem Esche, J., Mathwick, C., Novak, T. P., & Hofacker, C. F. (2013). Consumer power: Evolution in the digital age. *Journal of Interactive Marketing*, 27(4): 257–269.

Lee, S. (2017, March 1). 2016 Advertising Spending in Korea. *KAA Journal*, 46–47.

Lohr, S. (2012, February 11). Opinion-Big Data's Impact in the World. Retrieved February 10, 2018, from http://www.nytimes.com/2012/02/12/sunday-review/big-datas-impact-in-the-world.html

Magno, F., Cassia, F., & Bruni, A. (2017). "Please write a (great) online review for my hotel!" Guests' reactions to solicited reviews. *Journal of Vacation Marketing*, 24(2).

Nesamoney, D. (2015). *Personalized Digital Advertising: How Data and Technology Are Transforming How We Market*. Old Tappan, NJ: Pearson Education.

Nichols, W. (2013). Advertising Analytics 2.0. *Harvard Business Review*, 91(3): 60–68.

Okazaki, S., & Taylor, C. R. (2013). Social media and international advertising: theoretical challenges and future directions. *International marketing review*, 30(1): 56–71.

Powers, T., Advincula, D., Austin, M. S., Graiko, S., & Snyder, J. (2012). Digital and social media in the purchase decision process: A special report from the Advertising Research Foundation. *Journal of advertising research*, 52(4): 479–489.

Schultz, E., & Diaz, A. (2017, April 05). Pepsi is pulling its widely mocked Kendall Jenner ad. Retrieved February 01, 2018, from http://adage.com/article/cmo-strategy/pepsi-pulling-widely-mocked-kendall-jenner-ad/308575/

Shin, D. (2014). A socio-technical framework for Internet-of-Things design: A human-centered design for the Internet of Things. *Telematics and Informatics*, 31(4): 519–531.

Truong, Y., McColl, R., & Kitchen, P. (2010). Practitioners' perceptions of advertising strategies for digital media. *International Journal of Advertising*, 29(5): 709–725.

Tucker, C. E. (2014). Social networks, personalized advertising, and privacy controls. *Journal of Marketing Research*, 51(5): 546–562.

Wu, L. (2016). Understanding the impact of media engagement on the perceived value and acceptance of advertising within mobile social networks. *Journal of Interactive Advertising*, 16(1): 59–73.

Zammuto, R. F., & O'Connor, E. J. (1992). Gaining advanced manufacturing technologies' benefits: the roles of organization design and culture. *Academy of Management Review*, 17(4): 701–728.

WOOYEOL SHIN

Wooyeol Shin (Ph.D. University of Minnesota, Twin-Cities) is the chief researcher at the Korea Center for Investigative Journalism-Newstapa(KCIJ). His research at KCIJ has examined the emergence of digital newsroom culture and the changing nature of journalism ethics and practices. He has also developed a tool for measuring news impact for nonprofit news media. His research has appeared in various academic journals including *Journalism, Environmental Communication* and *Asian Studies Review*.

JIYOUNG HAN

Jiyoung Han received her doctoral degree in Mass Communication with a minor in Political Psychology from the University of Minnesota, Twin Cities. With a primary focus on the theories of social identity, she studies psychological mechanisms behind the polarizing effect of news media. Her research on this topic appears in the *Journal of Communication, Mass Communication and Society*, and *International Journal of Communication*. She teaches at the Scranton College at Ewha Womans University.

SEUNG SOO KIM

Seung Soo Kim is a full-time lecturer in cultural studies at Chulalongkorn University, Thailand. Kim received his Ph.D. in Media Studies in 2016 from the University of Colorado-Boulder. His dissertation *Imagining Religion and Modernity in Post-Colonial Korea* explores how the formation, mediation, and circulation of contemporary imaginaries about Korean Protestantism and Buddhism are closely entangled with new digital media technology, neo-liberal brand culture, colonial history, and the modern imaginary of universal and linear historical timeline. His research interests include religion and media, mediation, materiality, and multiple modernities. His publications include "Media" (co-authored with Dr. Stewart Hoover), in *Handbook of Religion and Society* (Springer, 2016) and "Authenticity, Brand Culture, and Templestay in the Digital Era: The Ambivalence and In-Betweenness of Korean Buddhism" (*Journal of Korean Religions*, October 2017).

HEEWON IM

Heewon Im (Ph.D. University of Minnesota, Twin Cities) is currently working at the Consumer Insight, The Nielsen Company Korea. Heewon's research focuses on how consumers use healthcare product information from various commercial and non-commercial sources to make their healthcare decisions. Particularly, her research has examined: (1) consumers' health information seeking through various media sources and its impact on their perceptions of health outcomes; (2) health promotion campaign message strategies and effects; and (3) media representation of healthcare products. Currently, she explores how her research can be applied in the healthcare industry by working at the healthcare market research industry. At GfK and Nielsen, she has been working on various pharmaceutical and consumer healthcare projects from oncology to vaccines. At the same time, she continue her academic works: Her recent publication includes H. Im & J. Huh, "Relationship Between Exposure to Direct-To-Consumer Prescription Drug Advertising (DTCA) and Patients' Belief Accessibility and Medication Adherence" (*Health Communication*, 2018), and H. Im & J. Huh, "Does Health Information in Mass Media Help or Hurt Patients? Investigation of Potential Negative Influence of Mass Media Health Information on Patients' Beliefs and Medication Regimen Adherence" (*Journal of Health Communication*, 22(3), 2017).

BOHYEONG KIM

Bohyeong Kim received her Ph.D. in Communication at the University of Massachusetts Amherst. She will start a new position in August 2018 as Assistant Professor in the Department of Communication Studies at Vanderbilt University. Her research focuses on digital media, moral economy, and financial culture. Her work has appeared in *Cultural Studies* and the *International Journal of Communication*. She is currently working on a book manuscript about the digital cultures of wealth-tech in South Korea.

CHANGWOOK KIM

Changwook Kim (Ph.D. University of Massachusetts Amherst) is Assistant Professor of Sociology at Handong Global University. His research interests include creative industry, creative city policy, digital/creative labor, and cultural policy, specifically in East Asia. His research has appeared in various academic journals including *Television & New Media* and *the International Journal of Cultural Policy*. His dissertation entitled "*Assembling Creative Cities in Seoul and Yokohama: Rebranding East Asian Urbanism*" recently won the Best Dissertation Award from the Global Communication and Social Change Division of the International Communication Association.

TAEMIN KIM

Taemin Kim (Ph.D. University of Minnesota) is an assistant professor at Incheon National University in Korea. He was an assistant professor at Fayetteville State University in the U.S. With an interest in advertising and consumer psychology, his research explores the effects of advertising messages and brand communications in social media. In particular, a primary focus of his research is on the effects of warm messages on brand evaluations in the advertising and social media contexts. He previously was a global brand manager at LG Electronics and an account executive at Phoenix Communications in Korea.

KYUNG-HEE KIM

Kyung-Hee Kim (Ph.D. Ewha Womans University) is a professor in the School of Media and Communication at Hallym University and the director of the Institute for Communication Arts and Technology (iCat). Her research focuses on the interplay of digital culture, news organization, and gender. She has written and edited several books on social media, media literacy, and gender. She has also published in numerous journals including *Journal of Computer-Mediated Communication*, *Media, Culture and Society*, and *Asian Journal of Communication*.

한림대학교 **정보기술과문화연구소(iCat)**는 미디어 기술의 발전이 열어갈 사회의 변동과 문화의
미래에 대한 연구를 통해 사회발전의 방향을 가늠하고 대안을 제시하는 역할을 수행합니다.

한울아카데미 2078
ICT 사회 연구 총서 4

Digital Korea
Digital Technology and the Change of Social Life

ⓒ 신우열 외, 2018

엮은이 신우열, 김경희, 김창욱
지은이 김보형, 김승수, 김창욱, 김태민, 신우열, 임희원, 한지영
펴낸이 김종수
펴낸곳 한울엠플러스(주)
편집 최규선

초판 1쇄 인쇄 2018년 6월 11일
초판 1쇄 발행 2018년 7월 2일

주소 10881 경기도 파주시 광인사길 153 한울시소빌딩 3층
전화 031-955-0655
팩스 031-955-0656
홈페이지 www.hanulmplus.kr
등록번호 제406-2015-000143호

Printed in Korea.
ISBN 978-89-460-7078-3 93300

※ 책값은 겉표지에 표시되어 있습니다.

이 저서는 2015년 정부(교육부)의 재원으로 한국연구재단의 지원을 받아 수행된 연구임.
(NRF-2015S1A5B4A01037022)